THERE'S NOTHING WRONG WITH GERMANY...

BUT HERE'S 50 THINGS YOU'LL NOTICE

BY PAUL HUGHES

Germany is a beautiful country full of amazing people, infrastructure, towns and cities. I often feel the country gets a bad rap, owing to the way people perceive Germany based on a reasonably disastrous period of its history from around 1918 - 1945. While these years live on in the memory of those who experienced it, it will always continue to cast a shadow over an industrious people, with a robust work ethic and strong family values.

However, its leadership in Europe is beginning to replace those memories with newer and better ones. Germany's compassion for those fleeing the Middle East following the violence and problems there have also been highlighted on the world stage.

This book is a lighthearted collection of things I have personally noticed and experienced since I moved here as an Englishman in 2015, and married a German. It is the quirks and observations that I have noticed, making Germany as unique, as it is beautiful.

Contents

Part 1
Introduction

Me in 2018 in Wiesbaden, Germany. I am probably looking at something German, like a Dachshund, or a liter of beer, or a Schnitzel, or a Dirndl, or, well, you get the stereotypes.

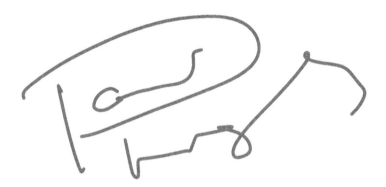

First off allow me to start by saying how appreciative I am that you have taken your time to purchase, borrow, or steal a copy of this book. Either electronically, or good old-fashioned paper.

It has taken me around five years to write this, though obviously not all at once. It's not like I have been doing nothing other than incessantly tapping at a keyboard for the last five years, that would require at least two things that I am not famed for, dedication and focus.

This is in fact, at least my fourth attempt to write a book. The first time I tried, it was a book about coaching and improving your life. At the time I had recently qualified as a life and business coach. I had studied Neuro Linguistic Programming (NLP) for around two years and secretly believed that I had found the hidden recipe for success and happiness and set about trying to share that wisdom.

I really enjoyed learning the art and science of this fascinating subject and wanted to share my newfound wisdom via a book. That book got to around 80% complete and sits on my iCloud gathering... computer dust? Either way, when I came back to it with a view to releasing it a few years ago, I was able to read it through the eyes of a potential reader and the whole thing felt a little *preachy.* So I left it where it is, in the annals of a cloud computer somewhere. Which is a shame, because I did pour many hours of my life into it.

The second effort was around how to stand up and speak in front of people. As part of my professional career, prior to taking up a Multimedia career, I was amongst other things; a customer service representative, sales manager, project manager, account manager and training manager. Until I essentially burned out, packed it all in and fled to Europe.

Throughout most of my career I was in a management position, and those jobs required me to possess a ninja like ability to whip up a PowerPoint presentation, often under incredible duress and with ludicrous turnaround times. I was always adept at finding ways to present an idea, or a concept to people and along the way; I became a reasonably good speaker/presenter.

I enjoyed those parts of my jobs the most and eventually it led to me becoming a Radio DJ. I went by the moniker "Paul the Brit" and for three years I would wake up at 5 a.m., every morning to present the morning show on the American Forces Network in Wiesbaden, Germany.

It was during this time that I created my own courses on how to speak publicly, which became the motivation for my second attempt at a book. That book called "Terrific Talking" is about 30% finished and also sits on my iCloud gathering computer dust.

My third attempt was actually the first attempt I made to write this book. Back then I just ran out of steam. But this time... and by virtue of the fact that you are reading this, it was obviously completed!

If you don't want to learn about my journey, and me, preferring instead to just skip to the 50 things I have noticed, you can leap forward to page 20. If you are curious, then please do turn the page for the introduction.

Getting to Germany

I grew up in a very non-aspirational town. It is the kind of town that everyone in the UK has heard of, but has never actually been to.

Swindon, in the South West of England, is a town that people know the name of, but don't necessarily recall why. Most likely it's because they have driven along the Motorway M4, between Bristol and London at some point. Swindon can be seen from this main artery road that joins London to Cardiff in Wales.

Swindon is mainly famed for two things: Isambard Kingdom Brunel, one of the UK's greatest ever engineers and father of the railway system, and roundabouts. Specifically, the magic roundabout, you can Google it; it's the first result!

My house was your typical terraced house, which you will find in streets all over Britain. It's a row of red brick houses, in blocks of 20, with two floors, three bedrooms and downstairs bathrooms. In front of each house was a small square "garden" the width of the house and maybe 4 feet deep. This is where you would store your rubbish bins. Meaning that when you drive down the street, nearly every house has an overflowing garbage can in front of it. Failing that, the front gardens would be full of rubbish that people would lob into it as they walked past.

Inside, I shared a small bedroom with my brother, whom is only 15 months younger than I am. This arrangement continued for most of my teenage life, until at the age of 16, my parents "kindly" cleared out the spare "bedroom." This room had never even contained a bed and given that there were 4 people in the house wasn't really "spare" either. The room was essentially used as a junk room and remained permanently filled with crap for most of my young life.

The room was so small that you couldn't even fit a single bed into it. Therefore I had 5'7 child's bed and I am 5'11 tall. Prison cells are actually bigger than my bedroom and less damp. But at the time I didn't care, it was mine.

My prison cell was located at the backside of the house overlooking our very large, very badly kept garden. This was a permanent source of amusement to many of our families' friends, because my mother was a professional gardener. Or so she said. At the end of the garden was an enormous four-car garage, which my dad built to house his collection of American cars and hotrods, which he restored himself. On dark winter nights after school, he would teach us how to build cars and we would don tiny mechanics overalls to ensure we didn't get our clothes dirty while helping out. Our assistance mainly amounted to fetching spanners for him, whilst he led under the car with his legs sticking out, cursing.

Beyond the garage I could see from my window the jewel in the crown of my childhood, St Mark's Park. St Mark's wasn't a large park, but to a kid, it was huge. This park was everything to me; it was the social center of the world. We were allowed to play anywhere within the boundaries of the park. This was fine because, it had tennis courts, a recreation center, a pond, wooded areas, football pitches and a play area with a huge spider web contraption, which was over 30 feet tall. It was the epicenter of many childhood misadventures.

We very rarely ventured outside of the parks boundaries however, because my dad had an ability to produce a deafeningly loud whistle, the kind you can do when you stick your fingers into your mouth and blow. He would use these whistles as a warning siren that tea was ready, or it was time for bed and we would run home from whatever it was we were doing. The whistle could be heard in all corners of the park and if we couldn't hear the whistle, dad would know we were out of earshot and not in the park. To avoid getting in trouble we always stayed within the boundaries and many occasions we would run home after thinking we had heard it - just in case!

I went through everything in that park I learned to play football, rounders, cricket, tennis and rugby. I skateboarded, BMX'ed, got beaten up, beat others up, I fell out of trees and even accidentally burned down a small section of it one time.

Rain, shine, ice or snow we were out there, we knocked on our friends' houses from down the road to come out and play, and sprinted to the park to play football and get up to youthful shenanigans. I couldn't wait to get home from school, to get changed out of my uniform and go straight over the park.

Sadly, school and I never really got on. Sure, I can try and blame the school, the teachers or the content, but in truth, it was I. Not only was I largely unmotivated to learn, any motivation I had was usually directed at chasing a football, or girls.

The warning signs that my education was on the slide were all there, and it wasn't through a lack of effort on school's part to help me either. One day, after school my tutor sat me down. He wasn't a pleasant man and had a reputation of being a bit of a hardass. He was probably in his early 40's and completely bald on the top of his head, leaving only a line of hair around the base of his skull, which grew perfectly into his jet-black beard. It was 1996 and I had just completed my Mock Exams. These are the exams you do before your final year of school to get an idea of where you are at educationally. I, with some pride had managed to get straight C Grade passes. Brilliant, success! This was all I needed in my mind; it would be enough to get me into A-Levels and onwards for a career in the Royal Airforce as a Pilot! Job Done!

His warning however was stark. He advised me that my final exams in just over one years' time could go "either way". He was insinuating that I was not so brilliant and was in fact lucky to get eight straight "C" passes. He wanted me to know that if I didn't pull my socks up I was likely to slip into straight D's. For clarity, at this point in time in the British education system "C's" were considered passes and a "D" meant that while you didn't fail the exam, you didn't do enough to get an actual "pass worthy" mark, meaning you wouldn't get into A-Levels.

Either way, this was in direct contrast to the buoyed confidence I had on the back of my straight C's. "Ha yea right" I thought. "You watch me."

A whole year went by, where I was completely oblivious to my fate. I didn't see the danger signs that my education was being thrown away despite the fact that I rarely had any notebooks or course books. I never did homework and I didn't even carry a pen. But by that time, I was lost in a haze of blossoming puberty and girls that were blossoming into puberty.

Fast forward 18 months and I was walking away from school after visiting it for the last time to collect my GCSE results. I was nervous, but confident that I had succeeded. I didn't tear open the envelope right away whilst my fellow students around me loudly shared their successes and failures. I walked away from the school to open mine in private.

I cautiously opened the envelope expecting to see straight "C" passes, except for drama studies where I knew that I had flunked the written part of the exam. Thoughts of my tutor 18 months beforehand entered my head as I pulled out my results.

Turns out, he was right. I achieved one "C," seven "D's" and an "E". The "E" being for drama studies - about the only result I had expected. Effectively I had failed all of my GCSE's.

This failure put a bit of a spanner in the works of my plan to flee Swindon and join the Royal Air Force. I couldn't even get onto my selected college courses and had to face the indignity of taking my Math's and English exams again at college a year later, which, I again failed.

Giving up on education, I left college and what followed was at least 15 years of job-hopping and frustration - until I finally worked my way into a career in Multimedia - where pragmatism and creativity – skills not taught at school — are able to get you ahead.

I was lucky I suppose, that while I wasn't a particularly good student, I was – and still am— a good employee. Mostly. If you discount the time I got fired in the summer from my first real job.

That job was working in a call center answering calls for a company called Radio Rentals. Radio Rentals modus operandi was to basically allow people that were too poor to be able to afford a television, washing machine or VCR, the option of renting one. They would also rent you those goods if you were unable to get credit to buy those appliances, which gives you an idea of our customer base.

Included in the weekly rental price was a service contract where between the hours of 8 a.m. and 6 p.m., they could call up and request an engineer. We would arrange the dispatch for them to come out and fix their problem. Nine times out of ten, the problem was they had sat on their remote control and detuned the television. Now, unable to figure out why all the channels were showing that white noise screen your TV defaulted to, they would call me and request an engineer to come out and do it for them.

The job could be particularly challenging. Especially the times where you are trying to tell a 78 year old, mostly deaf woman, who lives alone, that it was going to take a week for an engineer to come and fix her TV. Which, since the TV was her only form of life, would likely be too late.

We sat in banks of ten in an open plan office, the walls reverberating with the chatter of over 150 agents talking to customers in various states of mental decay. The offices of the call center had no air conditioning, meaning in the summer it was disgustingly hot. My car however, did have air conditioning. After sweltering in my office all morning, talking to over 100 different callers, I decided I didn't want to go back. So, I spent an entire afternoon driving around the countryside, in refrigerated bliss, believing that no one would notice me gone.

They did, and they were not amused, or forgiving.

I did enjoy that job and it taught me the valuable skill of establishing rapport quickly with strangers. A skill that is of no use to me now I live in Germany, where there are far fewer polite, inconsequential social interactions. It's not that the people aren't friendly, they just appear to have no interest in conversing with strangers.

Whenever I go back to England, I am always amazed by the inane chatter I will have with shop assistants, people in queues, McDonald's etc. In Germany though, it never really happens, which is a good thing I guess, because my German is pretty dreadful. More on that, later in the book.

I have always been someone who enjoys work, making things better and moving on and up. The list of jobs I have had are endless, but the main constant throughout my career has been my need for constant change. I can stick a job about 8 months before I get the itchiest of itchy feet and need a new challenge. Something like a promotion, or a big project, or just to move on. This means I have a very diverse CV and consider myself a real "jack of all trades and master of none".

Throughout my career I have worked in many countries around the world including, Sweden, Poland, the Netherlands, the USA, Kuwait, Iraq (with the Royal Air Force Reserve), Scotland, Wales (OK these two are a gimme, but they count!) and finally Germany.

It all started when I met my now wife in London when working for a German logistics company. At the time she was an intern and I was a Business Development Manager. I feel it prudent to clarify that she was a mature intern... not like an 18 year old intern. In Germany all interns seem to be much more mature. Anyway, I was instantly attracted to her and through broken English email exchanges, we set up our first date.

When you grow up in England and you are from outside of London, you are taught that London is a busy, dangerous, nightmare of a place and to never go there - less ye face the nightmare of traffic, smog and getting lost.

Therefore, whilst I worked on the outskirts of London, my knowledge of the actual city was negligible. My future wife however did have a good knowledge of London, which was a lot better than her knowledge of English at that time. So whilst she navigated us around tube stops and sights, I navigated her around the English language.

11

She used to do this thing, where every time I said something, she would let out a stifled laugh. At first, I thought it was because she found me hilarious. I then realized it was because every time she didn't understand what I had said, rather than ask me what it was, she would just assume I was trying to be funny and let out a little laugh. She still does it to this day actually, although because I *am* hilarious, it's a lot more rare.

We have lived in Germany now for around five years and it was never our plan. We ended up here as a result of my wife's job, and the fact that I have ended up living in Germany still startles me. When I was younger, I never pictured living outside of my hometown, certainly not outside of England and never Germany!

When you look back on your life and try to string together how it is you got to where you are now, sometimes you can see a number of crossroads in your past. Every road you went down along the way, had to be taken exactly how you took it, in order for you to get to where you are right now. I have reflected on this a few times and thought, "well if it wasn't for making that decision, I wouldn't be there," and "if I hadn't made the decision before that, then I wouldn't have even gotten to that point anyway".

So, as I sit here typing this in Germany, trying to trace my life back so I can understand just how I got to this point, I can see one of the main "crossroads" of my life was navigated sometime in 2002. This was the year I joined British Armed Forces and signed up to the Royal Air Force Reserve.

My father had served in the RAF as a ground electrician repairing hospital equipment in Air Force Hospitals, that have all long since closed. My father had to leave the forces and cut his career short, when my mother left him after having an affair. I was around three years old and my brother had just turned two. My father made the decision to leave behind the forces, to take care of my brother and I. He ended up working nights in a factory making wire and cable for many years.

We had relocated back to Swindon, to the same street, only two houses up from the house my father and his three sisters had grown up in. We would grow up going to the same school and playing in the same park, that he had when he was growing up.

It is in part down to him that I had always dreamt of being in the RAF. My poor schooling performance meant that I couldn't get into any of the trades I wanted and was ultimately refused entry. That failure ate away at me every day while I toiled in jobs that were repetitive and unfulfilling. It led me to constantly question, what it was I was going to do with my life.

I had clung to the dream of joining the RAF from my earliest memory – even in Primary school – and it was around my 13th birthday when I joined the Air Cadets. A uniformed youth organization for those that have an interest in the military or serving in the armed forces later in their lives. I loved my time in the Air Cadets, flying, shooting, going on camps and I even loved the discipline to an extent. It gave me a taste of what my potential military life could be.

Despite not getting into the Air Force, I was still intent on serving my country. I even applied to join the Army at one point and later I did join the RAF Reserves. I didn't just want to be a reservist though; I wanted to do all I could to integrate into the full time RAF.

A full two years of training later and I was proudly wearing my blue beret and RAF cap badge. It meant so much to me to finally be in uniform and straight out of training, I volunteered to be mobilized into active service.

The year was 2007, and at the time the UK was fighting two wars simultaneously. The British Armed Forces were still in Iraq and were now fighting in Afghanistan with NATO. Manpower was sorely needed and I was mobilized almost straight out of training. My initial call up was for a period of 6 months at RAF Brize Norton, in Oxfordshire. Brize is the main logistics hub for the RAF. I worked on the cargo section for six months preparing aircraft loads that included vehicles, ammunition, general freight and luggage, ready for loading onto the aircraft.

I loved the lifestyle and took to it like duck to water. I moved onto the camp and got given a tiny room in the barracks, not much larger than my old spare bedroom, prison cell and not as nice. But this time, a full size bed at least. There was only one working shower for 15 men and the heating didn't work. Despite that I was happy.

I was working 12-hour shifts, on a four on, four off pattern. The first 2 days were 6 a.m. to 6 p.m., and then you would "swing" over to nights and work 6 p.m. to 6 a.m. We would treasure the times we got "stood down," which is where they have more manpower than work and at midnight you could go home to enjoy almost four and a half days off.

When my time at Brize Norton neared its end, I began to dread that I would soon have to go back to my civilian job. My job at that time was as an Account Manager; where I worked supplying defense and other manufacturing firms with grey-market, obsolete electronics. The grey-market for electronics existed because, let's say you have an aircraft built by Boeing in 1982, the electronics that aircraft utilizes are long since obsolete - the manufacturer simply stopped making them decades ago as technology advanced. Manufacturers are unable to simply buy that component from a store, or distributor. Since it would be too expensive to design, manufacture and test a new component that replaces the faulty part, they would call us.

My job was to scour the globe to find the part, sometimes costing upwards of two to three thousand dollars apiece from distributors and companies that had surplus stock. When I found the component, I would buy it, mark it up and sell it to the defense contractor. I loved it; I just didn't particularly like my colleague.

Cara was a semi pretty, blond bobbed, short, stuffy woman, who was, for the most part a very lonely woman. Her last boyfriend had left her a decade before and her only companion in the world was her cat, who probably also hated her. Cara was a complete sociopath and I could not bear the thought of having to go back and work with this woman and as it turns out, I wouldn't have to.

I received a request to go and visit my commanding officer (CO) at my headquarters squadron. This was a square building of many small rooms, built somewhat unceremoniously in the 1950's. Originally, it was a barracks block that housed single soldiers. Every room was – in its former life – a bedroom and every three rooms or so was a bathroom, with a full bath and shower installed. The weirdest office.

I hadn't been back to HQ since the start of my mobilization, and I was a little worried about why they wanted to see me. Generally it is never good when your CO wants to see you.

When I arrived, I was called into a small stuffy office that was in its previous life someone's bedroom and as it turns out, I wasn't in trouble. Instead, I was asked if I could extend my mobilization. Excitedly I responded, "Yes Sir".

As much as I didn't want to go back to working with Cara, I was also loving my life in the Air force. The CO smiled at my eagerness to extend and asked if I was sure, because extending my mobilization would mean joining up with the British forces in Basra... in Iraq... In the middle of summer... Where temperatures would regularly exceed 50 degrees centigrade.

Not only that but the contingency operating base (COB) in Basra, was under constant enemy rocket attack. I said again, "Yes, Sir".

So, as a result of this I ended up volunteering to go to Iraq in 2007, another crossroads.

That four months at war in the desert, was the toughest four months of my life. The pace was relentless, 12-hour days, seven days a week, for months. The heat would get so intense your brain couldn't really process it, I had never felt anything like it. You know when you're cooking and you open the oven and that whoosh of heat hits your face? It was like that, only all over your body and every time you move, or the wind blows you burn. The sweat runs in rivers down the back of your knees and into your socks. You have to drink water constantly to try and keep up with the fluid you lose. Thankfully, after I arrived, I was told I would be on the nightshift where temperatures would *only* be around 40-45 degrees.

I was responsible for loading and unloading allied aircraft like the C130 Hercules transporters and the massive C-17 globe master, recently purchased by the RAF. We would load and unload freight, vehicles, explosives or "bang" as it was called by us, at all hours of the day or night.

When I first arrived I just could not get my head around the incredible heat. We had to wear our uniform at all times, and when working on the aircraft we had to wear our body armor and helmet as well.

Our section – which heavily relied on a multitude of vehicles to be able to move freight to and from the aircraft – was in the middle of the airfield, which other than the paved areas, is essentially desert. Some of our vehicles weighed up to seven tons, so to prevent the vehicles getting stuck in the sand; our working area used inter-locking steel sheets, which would be laid on the desert floor. They did somewhat of a good job in enabling us to drive our vehicles without sinking into the sand.

One major problem with these steel sheets however, was when the attack siren rang out. When this happened, as it did multiple times a day, you had to throw yourself down onto your face, as lying prone was the safest way to avoid being blown up. The siren would go off sometimes two to three times a day. The sirens were warning us that rockets had been fired at the base. These rockets had been picked up by our radar system and triggered the alarm. When the radar system didn't detect the rockets though, your only warning of an attack was an explosion!

So, the attack alarm goes off, you leap out of the vehicle onto your face just before the first explosion, only to realize that these steel panels had been sat baking in the midday sun all day. The air temperature alone was 50 degrees centigrade and these steel panels would be as hot as a burger grill. So hot were they, that throwing yourself onto your stomach would cause you to get third degree burns, scalding your hands and arms, even your skin through your t-shirt. Of course this was all preferable to being hit by a rocket, but only just.

Safe to say, I survived my tour and when it finished, it felt like another crossroads in my life. I was glad to be home in one piece and I was full of optimism and life. I quit my job the first day back in the UK, even though I had no idea what I was going to do next and how.

I could see that going to Iraq had helped me get out of a deep depression that I didn't know I was in. I had been drinking daily for many years, as most people did that I knew. Those four months however stopped the cycle of binge drinking and misery that I had been locked into. It changed my life and helped me make better choices that would affect my future.

More crossroads included; breaking off my long-term relationship of seven years, meeting the mother of my child and having a son, then eventually, choosing a job that would cause me to meet my wife. After all that, and several other major life choices, including leaving the UK and living for a period in Amsterdam, I ended up here in Germany.

When we first came to Germany, I lived in Frankfurt, which for a small town boy was an enormous pile of ugly buildings built after the war that lack soul and character. It was quite intimidating with all the bank skyscraper buildings, speeding cars, multi-culture and confusion. I never really warmed to Frankfurt, feeling more like an alien than at any other point in my life. We had moved to Frankfurt from Amsterdam, where despite also being an alien, everything felt more welcoming and friendly.

Frankfurt is where I began to write down the things I noticed about German culture. It was not only a way to help me integrate, but also as something to occupy me as I looked for work.

During this time, I found a volunteering position at the American Forces Radio Network in Wiesbaden, the only English language radio program in the region. I volunteered full-time for nearly a year, when they managed to find a way to hire me. I worked as a Radio Presenter for nearly three years. It was the best job I ever had and I miss it to this day.

My job today is, as I like to call it, a "Content Creator" I make videos, take pictures, create graphics and write. I enjoy the multifaceted parts of media creation and it suits my "jack of all trades" nature.

After five or so years in Germany, I believe it is time to finally put out into the world the things that I have noticed. I have some reasonable experience of the people and its culture and it's time to share it. It is almost with a sense of relief that I finally type these words and to have the privilege of sharing my observations of this country that I have grown to love and respect.

I continue to live in Germany and will do so for the foreseeable future. I will continue to make friends with its people whom, out of all of the Europeans I have met, are closer culturally to the UK than any other country. I have found that Germans work hard and take pride in their work. It's why something being made in Germany is synonymous with quality. It's because, to a man, from pencil makers, to CEO's being proud of and taking pride in your work is as quintessentially German as moaning about the weather is for the British.

What follows are a collection of things I have noticed over the years, that are different enough from what I am used to, so much so that they stand out. Some of them are stereotypes that you may have heard of before, but they are all things that make Germany unique.

Some of the posts in the book are based on my Blog "the top 100 things I noticed about Germany," which I have been curating and adding to over the last five years since I arrived in the country. This book is a collection of my favorite of those 100 things, plus many that I have written especially for the book.

Part 2

50 things to notice about Germany

Lifestyle

Schlaf Gut!

Hotels in Germany are generally of a high standard. Very clean, decorated for function and with two or three things you will notice that still to this day strike me as odd.

Firstly and most annoyingly they have these enormous, fluffy, clean, inviting looking pillows in every hotel that contain NO filling.

In a country that produces the world's best cars, some of the world's best electronics and arguably the best tasting sausage, I would not have believed that something as basic as a pillow would be something a country could get so wrong. But here we are.

When you travel to a lot of hotels in other countries, there is a pillow or two on the bed and probably a spare pillow in the wardrobe. And if the pillows on the bed are too soft, you remove the spare pillow from the wardrobe. It is not a giant hardship. In Germany though, you will receive a single pillow, which is the size of two pillows, and it will be filled with... well... nothing.

These pillows are impossible, no matter how many times you fold it, stuff it, or move it around; the pillow is just absolutely useless. So you can either face a week of playing pillow origami, not sleeping and waking up with a giant crick in your neck, or do what I do. Take your own.

While my taste in pillow differs from that of your average German, there is a saving grace for their hotels. Couples the world over have fought, argued and screamed about their other half stealing the Duvet, or hogging the middle of the bed (a favorite hobby of my wife's).

But... while the "pillow designing" Germans were on a day off, the "how can I avoid duvet related murder" Germans were on hand to solve this problem. The solution they created is a remedy so simple; it could be considered genius... if you order a double room in Germany, you will find the double bed appears to be a normal double bed, but it has two single duvet covers, neatly folded at the bottom of two single beds.

The battle is over and you can sleep well now. That is if you remembered to bring your own pillow.

Schönen Feierabend!

Schönen Feierabend is one of my favorite German sayings.

It has no direct translation to English, but it roughly means "Have a nice evening". But it doesn't. In fact, Feierabend is the period of time after leaving work, but before you get home. For instance, you leave work at 5 and head to the pub for a beer with colleagues before going home, this is your Feierabend.

You may be asked for a Feierabend Bier, by your colleagues, which is the English equivalent of "a quick pint"

Prost!

Prost if you're a German, or "Cheers" if you are from the US or UK.

Germans do like beer, which is perhaps one of my favorite things ever, and when coupled with a sausage, I am in Bavarian heaven.

Germany has a long tradition of great beer and you will find a much bigger selection of beers here than anywhere else on earth. With so much choice and with such high quality, you could drink a different beer every day for 19 years, before you tried the same beer twice! Wheat beer (Weizen) in particular is delicious.

In order to know the correct beer drinking etiquette you need to know that, when you join a German for a drink, it is very usual to toast, (as it is in the UK only far more often,) and you need to replace cheers with "prost".

The good drinking etiquette doesn't end there though, there is one marked difference. In Germany according to tradition, you are supposed to look the person in the eye when you "chink" your glass with that person. Even if you are "prosting" with a large group. You must go through each member of the group chinking glasses and making eye contact.

The legend says that if you do not do this, you will face seven years of bad sex. Germans will often toast several times throughout the drink, so it can be a fairly time-consuming process.

It is particularly uncomfortable to "Prost" your girlfriend's father, whilst he demands you look him in the eye... I know that he does not wish himself to have bad sex, but in a roundabout way he is ensuring his daughter doesn't either... CHEERS!

Open a Beer with ANYTHING

You have probably been there - hot summer's day, nice picnic spread and a couple of bottles of beer. But then, uh oh, no beer opener!

This will normally lead to you trying to open the beer on trees, walls, or anything else hard within reach. The end result of which is you chipping the bottle and risking death or serious injury from consuming your cold, refreshing beer with added glass. Or you might just give up altogether.

Well, this is literally **never** going to be a problem if you are with a German. You see Germans can open bottles of beer with ANYTHING. I have seen beers opened with lighters, keys, credit cards, coins, horns, back scratchers, saws, hammers and even **ANOTHER BEER**.

I think this was the pinnacle of my German integration. The day I successfully learned how to open a bottle of beer with another bottle of beer and it's now my party trick.

For the curious, – here's how it is done:

1. Grasp the beer you want open around the top of the neck, with your knuckle right up near to the bottle cap

2. Take the other beer and hold it in your right hand around the middle and turn it upside down

3. Place the beer caps together with the top beer cap positioned under the bottom bottle cap and using your left index finger hold the bottle tops together

4. Squeeze tightly and lever the beer in your right hand down, using your knuckle as a fulcrum

5. If you are holding it tightly enough, the lever action will pop open the beer in your left hand, leaving the lid of the beer in your right hand intact

6. Enjoy the feeling of being ALL MAN

7. Consume delicious beer

You're welcome!

Oh! You are English!?

The British overseas are in actual fact quite a rarity. Outside the sun kissed areas of Europe such as Spain, Portugal and the south of France, you will seldom come across a British ex-pat.

Germans who can speak English, like to speak English. In large cities, as a Brit, you may need to prepare yourself to be accosted by drunks, random weirdo's and colorful students whom, upon hearing you are native English will spend the next 5 minutes earnestly practicing the only English they know with you.

In Frankfurt I would have near daily conversations that were exactly the same. These friendly people would slur their way through their high school English and then fumble around for sporadic words that make no intelligible conversation.

I'm not really complaining, in fact I rather like it. And if they weren't invariably drunk, or crazy, I would think it was cool that people so willingly dive into English. Sometimes make you feel like a minor celebrity, such is the rarity of the native Englishman in Germany.

Street Drinking is OK

In contrast to the UK and most of the US, in Germany, it is largely OK to drink in public.

A German friend of mine was enjoying a nice beer on the tube in London one time. Rounding off a splendid Feierabend, only to be accosted by the British Transport Police, whereupon he was told to dispose of the contents. Imagine his surprise, as only two weeks earlier he had been doing the exact same thing in Germany with no problem whatsoever.

Watch out for Saturday afternoons where local supporters of football clubs commuting to and from stadiums, will be celebrating victory – with a beer, or drowning their sorrows after a loss – with a beer.

Crowds and queues

Germans may never master standing in a queue, but they are undoubtedly masters of the "general melee".

It makes the blindest bit of difference if you are lining up patiently at a bank, or store, because Germans can be completely oblivious to the social order I'm familiar with.

More than once a German has wandered straight past the line of people, stood orderly and patiently, right up to the server. Then – totally deaf to my tuts and exasperated huffs – they approach the counter, totally destroying all notion of order.

It's in stark contrast to where you would expect there to be no order at all, such as in crowds at music gigs for instance.

I have been to hard rock, punk rock, indie rock and electro rock gigs all over Germany, and my experience is largely the same. They don't push or crush to the stage, they stand reasonably spaced, in a general group and between songs, and they might even clap. Germans at gigs are largely motionless and reasonably spread out. It's as if they have been taught how to stand politely in a crowd and just assumed that this is the same discipline to use when queuing in store.

To be honest, I am still not used to it, being in a rock concert venue that holds 2500 people and getting more order and room than that time I was trying to hold together a queue with 25 people at a bar.

I'm Not Sorry

Sorry, sorry, excuse me, SORRY, could I just get by? A common word to an Englishman is "sorry". It is the go to word for all manner of purposes.

It is used for excuse me, trying to interject into a conversation, a polite dismissal of a mishap and even giving a genuine apology. Sorry is multi-functional. In England.

German people do not apologize anywhere near as much as the English, or Americans for that matter. When I travel back to England now, I am actually amazed at just how much time I spend apologizing for things – my fault or not.

When I first met my German wife, she told me off for apologizing too much, claiming, "I did not mean it." But of course I meant it! As an Englishman, I am pre-programmed to apologize all the time. But now maybe I agree with her, perhaps I did apologize too much.

Nowadays I say sorry less often, but still find myself apologizing as a matter of course. If a German bumps into you, cuts you off, or disagrees, you should not expect to hear an apology and you offering one will be met with complete indifference. Maybe it is because the German word for sorry is so horrendously convoluted? *"Entschuldigung!"* is the word, but of course owing to the German language there are at least 97 variations of the word, depending on who you are talking to, what you are apologizing for and whether or not it is being used as a verb etc.

Sorry, but it seems that due to my Germanification, I am no longer as sorry.

Rules Rules Rules!

One thing I will most likely never get used to is the rules.

There are lots of rules, many unwritten and some more obvious such as; don't cross the road unless the man is green. Never walk your dog without a leash. Never queue in an orderly fashion.

One time, I asked for an extra shot of Espresso in my Latte at a small local coffee shop. The reply was distinctly German.

"No, I am sorry, this is not allowed"

I tried to clarify that; I didn't want a free shot, just an extra one. But my German isn't really strong enough to carry through an argument. It's barely strong enough to order a coffee in the first place. I would have thought though that small local coffee shops would be more flexible, not less. But here - Das ist verboten (forbidden)

Another example is that when it snows, you are meant to clear the snow from any public paths directly outside your house. If you fail to do so and someone injures themselves, you can be liable under the law.

When you live in a shared house there is a roster, if it is your week and it snows, you clear the path. One night, my wife and I were out walking late and it snowed. Being that we were already out in our winter gear and despite it not being our week on the roster, we thought we would be nice and clear the snow.

The next morning, we get a knock at the door where an argument ensues about the fact that we had not adhered to the roster and cleared the snow and that we "shouldn't do that, it's against the rules"!

It's not just the existence of rules though; it is also the German's willingness to police each other to ensure that everyone sticks to the rules.

I can see the point, if everybody is policing each other, then society can safely function. As opposed to somewhere like Britain where it is polite to mind your own business, quietly tutting at the world as it burns.

No Fireworks!

Buying fireworks in Germany is largely impossible except for four days of the year.

In Britain from mid-October onward, you can legally buy fireworks from a raft of sketchy looking stores. These stores have imported container loads of explosives from China, for the local youth to buy and throw at each other.

In Germany however, fireworks are only sold at New Year's. Specifically from December 28, to Jan 1. It is not permitted to set off fireworks on any day other than New Year's Eve. The only exclusions are large festivals and professional displays.

In Britain, you will begin hearing fireworks from mid-October onwards. We have two main celebrations involving fireworks – Guy Fawkes Night on November 5 and New Year's Eve.

Stores however, will be open weeks in advance of this and as there are no laws protecting the peace and quiet like in Germany, you have to spend much of October and November listening to a recreation of down town Baghdad circa 2003.

In Germany, this means a quiet year all round particularly for pets, but this prohibition does mean that come New Year's Eve, every man, woman and child, is expected to blow something up. Meaning fireworks will be going for HOURS AND HOURS, a quick word of advice... since you can't beat them - join them.

Toilets

Toilets in many establishments I have frequented are subpar. Not only this, but in most places, you must also pay for the privilege of using the toilet. In shopping centers, restaurants and train stations you will have to pay the princely sum of 50 cents to relieve yourself.

I have always been of the opinion that you can gauge an establishment's overall level of hygiene by the cleanliness of its toilets. If the toilets are immaculate, then likely so is the kitchen.

When I'm not inspecting toilets for the cleanliness, I am normally making swift use of the facilities and the thing you will notice about a large number of toilet bowls in Germany is that it's very common for you to have to crap onto a shelf as pictured above. Apparently, the way German toilets are designed is to allow you to poo onto a ledge in the bowl, so that prior to flushing the water away you can examine your poo.

This is left over from the days where eating poorly refrigerated cold meats could leave you with worms or worse. Lovely.

Of course in the UK and for that matter, most places around the world, you crap into the water. This does a couple of things; it ensures that a particularly long poo remains relatively smell free, it also gives you some separation from your deposit when wiping.

My advice is to courtesy flush half way through. Crapping onto a small shelf is not a pretty sight, smell, or experience.

Iron Curtains

Houses in Germany look like the houses you will find all over Continental Europe, but different to those commonly found in the UK and the U.S. In England the houses in villages could be described as quaint, or cute. In Germany, you can describe them as functional, or bomb proof.

I live in an apartment built most likely in the 1950's and structurally it would survive everything but a direct hit from a 10 megaton blast. To keep out the sun and heat in the summer many German households have metal shutters on the outside of their windows, these also double as curtains. These shutters roll down like the security doors you see on the front windows of shops and obscure every particle of light from the outside. Coupled with this many apartments will have bars across the windows, to keep bad guys out in the summer.

My rear door, for instance, has a double glazed door, a fly net, a metal roller shutter and THEN iron bars with a lock. So, no one is ever getting in. But conversely, in a fire, how am I getting out??

Still, should WWIII ever happen, I probably won't even hear it.

Where's the Cooker?

A little something I was not prepared for and had never read anywhere prior to moving to Germany, is that when you rent or buy a place, the kitchen is generally not included.

Unless you have specifically agreed to buy the kitchen (around €2000) from the previous owners/tenants, the likelihood is that you will be moving into an empty room with some pipes sticking out of the wall.

So, when negotiating your let, remember to ask if the kitchen is included, or you may face an unexpected bill and a new best friend from the pizza delivery company.

No Hello

When you call a German on their mobile, or office number, if they don't recognize the caller, they will not ask "hello." They will just answer the phone directly with their surname.

It's efficient I guess, but is very strange to hear when that person has a one-syllable surname.

"Brrrrrrrrrp"

"HANS"

"Oh er, hello, is that Jurgen?"

I don't see what is wrong with pausing for a quick, "hello" at the start. It lets you know a conversation has begun, starting a conversation with your surname maybe cuts out a little waste, if you have accidentally dialed a wrong number, but as an "auslander" (foreigner) it doesn't inspire friendliness.

You also need to be aware that as the caller, you must introduce yourself by saying "Ja, Hughes, ist mein name, hallo" (yes, Hughes is my name, hello) – then launch into whatever it was you want to say.

50 Things to Notice about Germany

Culture

Thou Shalt Not Cross

Standing at a red light, on a cross walk, once all the cars are gone creates an interesting spectacle.

At any crosswalk, in a town, city or village, Germans can be found gathered at roadside, waiting patiently for the Green "Ampfelmanchen" to indicate that they are now allowed to cross the street. All very safe.

But, even if the road is completely devoid of cars and you can clearly see 200 meters in either direction that there is no traffic coming, they still won't cross. In actual fact - as opposed to using their own common sense, or survival instinct, as a means to safely get across the road, they will stand at the red crossing light until it turns green.

Attempting to cross the road on red will create looks of astonishment and bemusement, as the Germans repeatedly look at you, then the light to confirm it is still red, then back at you, nonchalantly using your own common sense to traverse an empty road.

Crossing on Corners

When you are at a junction intending to turn right or left, driving off on a green light doesn't always guarantee the road around the corner will be clear.

Driving around German towns and cities is not a laid back cruise. In fact it's a bit of a chore.

In most towns and cities, the roads are usually very busy and contain many disappearing, or merging lanes, "Einbahnstraßen" (one way streets) and crossings. As a motorist, you have to keep your wits about you at all times and ensure you are on hyper alert because, it's not just cars you are trying to avoid hitting. It's also pedestrians that will leap out in front of you at junctions and intersections.

I believe this peculiarity is unique to Germany, but I may be wrong. It goes like this: if you are at a junction and are turning right, as your light goes green and you pull away from the lights and begin your turn, it is highly likely that the green light has shown pedestrians that it's safe to cross. This means you will pull forward, begin your turn and stop as the pedestrians cross, once it's clear you can drive on. These crossing exist everywhere and are sometimes very tricky to spot, if you ever miss one, your first clue will be that pedestrian that's just bounced off your bonnet and over your roof.

Spazierengehen - Walking

To "Spazierengehen" is to be German. Not quite hiking, but more than a stroll. "Spazierengehen" after breakfast, before lunch, after lunch, before coffee, before beer, sometimes during beer too. It's called a "Weg beer"- a beer for the way.

Germany has some very beautiful countryside and the people quite rightly take every advantage of it that they can. To go wandering around the woods, or down one of the many lanes leading out through the fields is quintessentially German. Bonus German marks are awarded if you walk with both hands clasped behind your back in a kind of self-congratulatory handshake for taking the time to appreciate nature.

Going for a walk such as this is regarded as the highlight of a weekend. Ask a German what they did at the weekend and "Ich habe spazieren gegangen" (I went walking) would be a common reply.

Cigarette Advertising

Cigarette advertising died out in the UK many years ago and to see it so prevalent in such a forward thinking country is odd.

Walking through towns and cities you will see hundreds of advertising billboards - as you do in all major cities. Some advertise radio stations, or shopping centers, or city events. The kinds of things you would expect to see on billboards. However, more often than not they will show a beautiful couple, with enormous smiles, gazing longingly at one another whilst holding cigarettes.

To give you an idea of just how out of place this feels to a non-native, this kind of advertising has been banned in the USA since 1994 and in the UK adverts showing people smoking have been banned since 1986!

It's such a peculiar juxtaposition because these advertisements are still forced to show the enormous warning labels, saying something menacing such as "Rauchen kann tödlich sein" (Smoking can be deadly) but the two sexy people in the adverts look like they are having the time of their lives!

Germany sits at number 33 in global cigarette consumption per capita, with an average of 1480 cigarettes per adult, per year. The USA sits at number 57 on the list, at an average of 1083 cigarettes and the UK fares much better at number 74 with 826 cigarettes per capita.

Another interesting tid-bit that you will notice is that Germans actually consume mainly American brands of cigarettes. This is as a result of the post-war period where cigarettes were a form of currency. American GI's received a ration of cigarettes, whether they smoked or not and they used these in exchange of goods and services. As a result it is still these brands today that dominate the advertising – Marlboro, L&M, Pall Mall and Lucky Strike to name a few.

Does this kind of advertisement work for anyone? Are non-smokers going to think, "hmm, that looks great, I think I'll take up smoking"?

I honestly thought this kind of advertising died out with the Marlboro man... or is he still around?

Healthcare System

The German social healthcare system is quite different to the National Health Service (NHS). It more closely resembles the US system of healthcare.

In Germany, there is still a kind of state healthcare, meaning no one is left to die of something easily curable, or to bankrupt themselves in order to pay for an unexpected fall.

The healthcare system however, is not optional. It is mandatory for every citizen to have health insurance and payment is taken monthly from your salary before you get a chance to waste it on activities that will shorten your lifespan. Activities like smoking, drinking or eating fast food. Your healthcare payment is (at least according to Wikipedia) very good value for money. Not only does your employer pay 50% of your healthcare costs, the Euro Health Consumer index states that Germany has long had the most restriction free and consumer orientated healthcare system in Europe. Your health insurance will cost you around 15% of your annual income.

I can attest to the fact that healthcare accessibility is far better. Since I arrived here I have had CAT scans, counselling, physiotherapy, voice coaching, ear nose and throat specialists and much more than I may have got in the UK.

The paradox with the NHS seems to be that, you get sick and you make an appointment to see your doctor or GP, but you wait 2 weeks for that appointment, by which time you are feeling better anyway. This is partly down to the fact, in my experience that you must visit your GP for everything. Sore elbow? GP. Flu? GP. Ebola? GP. From there you will get referred to a specialist incurring another endless wait.

In Germany, it's a great deal less restricted, whilst you would in the first instance see your GP for most ailments, it's not always the case. If you have a problem with your back you can go straight to a chiropractor. Problem with your voice? Straight to the Ear Nose and Throat specialist. It will mean that you become less shy about going to the doctor, because you know that you are likely to see someone relatively quickly and can eliminate the step of seeing the GP.

One thing in particular you may notice though is the lack of "over the counter" remedies available in stores. In the rest of Europe basic healthcare items like paracetamol, cough syrup and basic medical supplies, are available in nearly every corner shop and fuel station. But this is not the case in Germany. Not only do you have to go to an Apotheke (pharmacy) for EVERYTHING, those basic supplies are also much more expensive.

I may be talking out of my arse, but I suspect the lack of a state healthcare system means a lack of competition, so pharmacies are able to charge more. Ibuprofen will set you back 4-5 euros compared to just pennies in the UK.

One other thing to note is that all but a couple of Emergency Apotheke's are closed on Sundays. So do not even think about getting sick on a Sunday.

Korn

Korn is simply the German word for "Grain" but the kind of Korn I am talking about is Kornbrand or Kornbranntwein.

"Korn" is a disgusting and highly potent form of alcohol, which is distilled from fermented cereal grain such as Rye, Wheat or Barley. It is in the same vain as spirits like Vodka, but is distilled to be a slightly (very slightly) lower alcohol proof and filtered less to retain the (disgusting) cereal grain flavor. Think of it as German Moonshine.

Many people believe Jägermeister is the stereotypical German national drink. However, I have lived in Germany over 5 years and have never drunk a single Jägermeister. In fact, up until recently, you rarely saw it in bars and clubs and when you did, it was ordered by tourists, not natives. But it is growing in popularity.

I have on several occasions (for some reason, I keep doing this to myself) had Korn shots. Normally it is at the end of a night, when I am already too drunk to be fully in control of my senses.

The best part is that upon waking in the morning, you will have a special type of hangover and those burps you get the day after a drinking session? Well, those burps are going to taste of Korn for the rest of the day. At least.

Don't try to get anything done on a Sunday.

German's take Sunday rest very seriously, you will not find any supermarkets open and 99% of all retail shops are closed. It is better you stock up on all the things you think you might need on the Saturday.

Sunday's are used instead for long lazy breakfasts and walks in the country side with no particular destination in mind. You will find some restaurants and bars may be open but don't plan on buying any DIY equipment, or food on a Sunday.

Weihnachtsmarkt (Christmas Markets)

Perhaps the single greatest thing that Germany EVER created. Better than Porsche, better than Sausage, maybe even better than beer, it is the adorable Christmas Market.

Big words, but believe me, Christmas markets are the greatest. thing. ever. Only those that have never been to one would disagree with me. By the end of November, nearly every small town in Germany will begin burdening their small market squares with little wooden huts, grand carousels, stages and lighting displays that are visible from space. The scene is set, all that's missing is the atmosphere.

Jam packed and open nightly from the beginning of December to Christmas eve, you can walk around these cute, kitsch little markets, that offer gifts you can't find anywhere else, meat from every animal and the best part of every Christmas market, Glühwein.

This tasty winter drink is a real treat. It is the English equivalent of Mulled wine, but without all the fuss. Warmed spiced red wine, often with a shot of brandy or rum added to it creates the perfect winter warmer for standing around on cold German nights.

Germans, incidentally also do summer wine festivals better than anywhere else and there are similarities between the two. For instance, you will find many of the same drinks at Christmas Markets, are the same drinks you drank at Summer markets, but just heated up. These may include: (and bear with me here, I have sampled most of these)

- Weisser Glühwein (Hot White Wine)

- Heisser Cider (Hot Cider)

- Heisser Tequila (Hot Tequila Shots (GROSS))

- Heisse Schokolade with Rum (Hot Chocolate)

- Glühkirschbier (Hot Cherry Beer)

These are just to name a few. If you find yourself passing through Germany in December, be sure to make it one of your stops. It will leave you full of Christmas spirit and cheer before you head back to the misery that is England in December, or America in December, or anywhere that isn't a small German town full of festiveness in December.

Christmas Eve

Come Christmas morning in Germany, the presents are already opened, Christmas dinner is already over and Christmas Day is all about... well, I still haven't figured that one out.

In Germany, the Christmas that I know of actually takes place on Christmas Eve. This is when it all happens and there are a few traditions that are different. For one, the Christmas tree is usually not even put up until Christmas Eve and is traditionally decorated with candles. Live flame and combustible Christmas decorations bring a real sense of danger, into an otherwise relaxing evening.

In the home of my wife, it is the father that prepares the tree – alone, with no one allowed to see. It is then unveiled to the family all at once. At the bottom of the tree is a small nativity scene, then the family gather around to sing Christmas carols together like "Stille Nacht, Heilige Nacht" (silent night, holy night) before exchanging a few modest gifts and then sitting down for a meal. It's not necessarily a traditional meal like in the UK or the US, where it is all about a plump bird, like turkey or goose. In Germany it can be almost anything.

I do find it a real contrast compared to the Christmases I had growing up. Traditionally there, Christmas Eve is about last minute shopping, wrapping up presents and meeting friends at the pub for a Christmas drink. Then the focus was always on the TV, before going to bed and waking up on Christmas Day where it all happens. Presents, Christmas dinner, maybe the pub again and then more TV, in the form of a James Bond re run on ITV.

In Germany on Christmas Day there will be a breakfast of meats and cheeses, maybe some Sekt (German Sparkling Wine) and coffee. Afterwards a walk around the local town or village is normally in order before returning home and playing games as a family. Card games or board games, it doesn't matter as long as my Father in Law is winning them. Then all is well.

"Hochzeit" The German Wedding

If you want proof that Germans work hard and play hard, look no further than a German wedding. If you ever have the opportunity to attend one, you simply must go. If not for the party, then for the free bar.

One way to bankrupt a newly married couple in the UK would be to have a free bar. Brit's wouldn't see it as a free bar, they would see it as an ALL YOU CAN DRINK bar. It would be a total disaster ending in multiple arrests and hospitalizations. The only reasons Brits stop drinking at weddings is because the bar closes or they run out of money.

For Germans, despite the bar nearly always being free, it is not about how drunk you can get. It's an alien concept for me, I don't remember most of the weddings I have attended due to beer related amnesia. Some habits die hard.

No such thing for most Germans, as they can really handle their drink. I mean it. I have never met a German I could out drink, it's like it is part of their DNA. I have been to several weddings and tried to keep up all night and every time without fail I have been in bed by 1 a.m., while the party continues without me into the wee hours. I then wake up the next day with a world ending hangover.

Our wedding was a small affair. We kept close to German traditions, including the one where the whole wedding procession, guests and all, honk car horns ALL THE WAY home from the church. Luckily for me it was just close family and friends, with the reception in my wife's parents' garden.

We borrowed a marquee, which would later collapse under the weight of the rain that fell on it, causing all of the table decorations that my wife had spent weeks thriftily preparing to be ruined. This forced us to move the whole party inside. It became a kind of wedding team building event.

Although we scrimped on infrastructure, one thing we didn't scrimp on was alcohol. We even rented a small bar with a beer keg to ensure a constant flow of happiness for our guests. We had wine, Sekt and spirits of all flavors. No one was running out of booze at my wedding!

We played traditional games and danced and sang and welcomed the local neighbors who brought gifts for us. Traditionally cash is given but rather than just hand over notes, it is actually given as part of what I would describe as a diorama - a small box with decorations where the money is hidden all around. Perhaps the Germans think an envelope of cash is tacky, but it is definitely a nice way to present a gift.

Gardening

In the UK, we have communal gardens located in the centers of cities and towns and they are called allotments. These remote gardens are extremely popular among people – generally, older people – who either do not have a garden, or only have a small garden. It gives them somewhere to grow food.

Allotments were made popular during the war, particularly during rationing, when the government put great swathes of land aside so that people could "Dig for Victory"

In Germany they have similar patches of land, generally in, or near busy cities, but they are used slightly differently. In Germany, they are actual gardens. They will most likely have a small shed containing a mower and other gardening tools, maybe some decking, a trampoline, a swing set, an apple tree maybe, usually a flag pole and it is completely fenced off.

It's funny to know that, when a German family would like to do something as simple as sit out in the garden, they are prepared to load the car and then drive several miles out of the city in order to do so.

Nudity

The German attitude to nudity is pretty liberal. The British attitude to nudity is not.

Ok, so let's be fair, it's not like you are going to turn up in Germany and start seeing boobs and dicks everywhere. It's not that extreme. But journey to a beach, or to one of the many swimming lakes dotted around the country and you are likely to see a "Freikörperkultur" (FKK) or "free body culture" area. A nude beach essentially.

This relaxed attitude to nudity is developed from a young age; nudity is not something to be ashamed of or hidden. As a result, when German children grow older, they are far more comfortable with nudity than the British, including me.

I learned all of the above in a "trial by fire" way. My wife wanted to take me to an enormous outdoor spa/sauna complex, with outdoor swimming pools, Jacuzzis and numerous saunas of various temperatures and sizes. It was the middle of winter and was snowing, which I am told is all part of the experience. With curiosity getting the better of me, I agree to go. Despite knowing I will have to be nude at various points.

When I arrived, I was pretty nervous, particularly at the point where you have to leave your bathing suit, or swimming trunks in a locker. You take only a towel and a robe to the bathing area and that's it. We haven't even left the changing rooms and I must have seen 5 pairs of breasts and at least 24 pairs of balls. Excluding my own.

Walking into a room full of naked people for the first time in your life, in your mid-thirties, is peculiar. Germans will make eye contact with you, they will say hello and like it or not, they will cop an eyeful. It seems to be accepted that everyone will look at everyone else – in fact hiding your modesty can cause grumbles amongst the unclothed. Better to just go along with it, you know, rules!

Initially, I sat with a towel covering my modesty, but after a few hours of being there, it does feel quite comfortable and natural... kind of. There is one or two notable exceptions though. People attend these kinds of places with their friends, colleagues and families! My reluctance to be naked in a room was balanced out by the fact that I would be in a room full of strangers. I couldn't imagine going to a place like this with friends, and friends' wives and partners. That would be too weird for my prudish ways.

The other part that felt peculiar to me was when a family walked in with two children. A girl aged around 14-15 and a younger boy maybe around 10. I am pretty sure by the age of 10 I was already aware of my nudity and would be horrified if my parents caught me nude, and my parents horrified if I caught them nude. I could not imagine ANY scenario where a self-conscious British 14-year-old, would follow their naked parents, into a room full of other naked people. German FKK – does take some getting used too.

Waiting Rooms

So, it seems that Germans greet each other in strange places, waiting rooms, elevators, and... sometimes toilets. But *always* in waiting rooms.

A small, sanitary white room with a cupboard for hanging coats in the corner. In the middle is a small table, full of German magazine publications, which, even if I could speak the language, I would, be unlikely to pick up to read anyway. The German equivalent of "Horse and Hound" I suspect.

Every few minutes, someone will enter and greet the whole room... "Guten Tag!" The whole room will respond in an echo "Guten Tag". Apart from me, that is... I find the whole thing rather strange. They do not say anything else to each other, only hello and good bye. Sometimes the informal way of goodbye "Tschüss" is used.

The direct translation of Tschüss is "See you again" which, judging by the amount of time I have already spent waiting, may actually be on their follow up visit in a week's time.

You called your baby what??

Traditional German names like Hans, Jürgen or Siegfried, have been steadily dying out over recent years and are being replaced by more "international" sounding names such as Ben, Leon, Paul or Tim. But what some people don't know is that when it comes to naming your baby, the Germans, whom stereotypically have a rule for everything, also have a rule for that.

The law states that you MUST be able to identify a baby's gender by its name. If you pick a neutral name, then the middle name must be the one that can identify its gender.

This would mean there could be no Ashley's, Alex's or Charlie's – all unisex names – without a middle name showing the gender.

This is particularly interesting, because Germany is one of the first countries in the world that has allowed for a third, or undefined gender on a birth certificate or identity document.

Dubbing

In many other European countries, western cinema is played in English and subtitled. This means that you can meet people from Sweden, Finland, The Netherlands etc. and they will speak remarkable English, albeit with an American accent, owing to all the US TV shows they consume.

However, in Germany, they dub over all English language movies and TV, with German actors and dub the film into German. In my opinion, what this does is potentially ruin great dialogue and movie scenes, because the words may have no direct German translation and it also creates an annoying visual where the mouths never match the words. It also has the Knock-on effect that Germans – many of whom speak two or three languages – have a very diluted exposure to British and American English.

I would be watching a film with my German girlfriend that starred an actor she had never seen in an original English film. Let's say Bruce Willis for instance. She would exclaim, "Oh my god, is that what he really sounds like?" Because in Germany you get used to the same voice actors, playing the same people. There is a German Bruce Willis, a German Arnold Schwarzenegger, a German Scarlett Johansson etc.

What a job that is, sitting around waiting for Arnie to make Terminator 14, so you can work again.

Qualifications

If you want to move to and work in Germany, you had better be qualified. Germans take qualifications VERY seriously and as a result, their whole education system is set up differently from that of the UK, or the USA.

Here in Germany, you either get a degree, or work as an apprentice in your chosen field to gain certification, this applies to nearly all jobs. This even includes historically low skilled jobs, like administration, or working in a bakery. It's not just formal trades, like plumbing or carpentry that are popular for apprenticeships, like in the UK.

Without an actual qualification, you will find it nearly impossible to be hired for a job. If you did somehow get a job without a qualification, but at a later stage want to go for a promotion, it is unlikely you would ever get the job over someone who has a relevant qualification – even if they had little, to no experience.

So how is it different in the UK at least? Well if you have 5 years' experience in Estate Agency, versus a University graduate with a relevant degree, your experience is pretty likely to be regarded by the employer as worth as much, if not more, than the degree. In Germany, the person with the qualification would get it.

The disadvantage I see to this, given my very diverse work history, is if you did an apprenticeship in something like Tax advising, then after 5 years want to do something else, essentially, you can't. You would first have to study and get qualified in order to move fields. I find the whole balance toward education frighteningly restrictive. But then I would, seeing as I am a dumbass, college dropout.

Hating Bayern Munich

As is the right of every football fan in the UK to hate Manchester United... other than Manchester United fans of course, it is every German's right to hate Bayern Munich.

One of Europe's most successful ever clubs, they have dazzled in recent seasons with amazing football, under great leadership from the likes of Louis Van Gaal and Pep Guardiola. They have won all competitions multiple times and boasted some of the greatest soccer players in world football, including Müller, Robben, Ribery, and Neuer.

In fact, much like Manchester United winning many Premier League titles over the last 15 years, Bayern Munich's domestic domination has been similar. At the time of writing it's nine titles in 15 years and this has resulted in their success becoming a little predictable. Bayern Munich fans have become well, arrogant. They don't just *want* to win, it's *assumed* they will win.

This is where the great German past time of "Schadenfreude" comes in. Meaning simply, "Pleasure in an others pain," everyone wants to see Bayern slip up, to lose a game they were not expecting, or to be dumped out of Europe. Unless of course, you are a Bayern Munich fan.

My advice? Don't be that guy. Go for Borussia Dortmund instead, everyone likes them.

What the Heck is Pfand?

The German Pfand (pronounced "FUND") system is a logistical marvel and newcomers nightmare.

Whenever you buy a drink, such as a bottle of cola, water, or beer, you will pay a small deposit on the actual bottle, or can each time. It's commonly either €0.08 or €0.25 added to the listed price of your drink. Once you return the bottles to a machine you get a little receipt, for the value of your returned bottles to spend in the store, in my case normally on more beer.

It is not just limited to shops though, at many bars and festivals that have outdoor seating, you will also pay a Pfand on your glasses, sometimes this is up to three euros per glass, refunded when you return the glass to them.

No matter how many times you visit a wine stand it's highly likely you will forget about this. Clutching a €10 note for your two €5 glasses of wine, only be told *(in German that you probably don't understand)* that your order costs €14 because you have forgotten to add Pfand again!

Not only is this system a necessity for Germany to have any hope of meeting their environmental targets, (it would be a lot of discarded plastic otherwise,) it also encourages you to recycle. Given the amount of bottled water you will have to buy living in Germany the Pfand will soon add up.

Because every bottle is worth a few cents, recycling also encourages cleaner streets. Many homeless (and sometimes not homeless people) will root through rubbish bins; in the streets and on trains looking for discarded bottles and cans to return in exchange for cash. Some rubbish bins even have holders on the outside of the bin to make it easier for them to collect.

Whilst overall, it is an inconvenience to haul these returns around, my favorite part about it is returning a shedload of bottles and getting enough Pfand back to cover the cost of my next crate of delicious German beer, it literally feels like free beer!

Cash Only Please

There are some places where Germany still hasn't caught up with the 21st century. One of those places is the banking sector.

Many restaurants, boutiques and kiosks will still not accept card transactions, despite technology now making this a very simple, cost effective practice in business. Whereas in the USA and the UK you can use your card to pay for any transaction, even down to using your card to pay for a 20p pack of gum.

The fact that Germany is still so heavily reliant on cash has caught me out on more than one occasion and will continue to do so.

Contactless payment, paying with your phone and even your watch may now be complete norms in other countries, but here every time you venture into a restaurant, you have to look around for signs of a card machine, or ask in advance to ensure you can pay for your meal. Otherwise you'll run into the dreaded "mit Karte?" "Nein!"

Fantastic, so now a walk to the nearest cashpoint (probably in the rain) to withdraw 20 euros to pay for the meal will be needed.

But that isn't where the frustration ends – because you see, there are *no* cash points. I come from a country where almost every petrol station, small store, and street corner has a cashpoint. Most department stores too. This is despite the fact you can pay for EVERYTHING WITH YOUR CARD ANYWAY. For an economy so reliant on cash as a means of transacting, why is it so hard to obtain?

When you do finally find a cash point, it probably doesn't belong to your bank – so if you do choose to withdraw your cash from it you will end up paying a fee... and not a small fee... these fees can be as much as FOUR EUROS & NINETY FIVE PENCE. Yes, five Euros to withdraw 20 because you do not bank with them... just to make clear my total astonishment with this, the UK abolished cash machine charges between banks back in the 1920's (probably).

So a top tip, always carry sizeable amounts of very stealable and loseable cash in your pockets on nights out and to restaurants, otherwise you could be facing a lengthy walk and a lofty charge for your ignorance.

Sie and Du

German is not an easy language to learn, anyone who has tried for longer than five minutes will know this. One of the main peculiarities is the Sie and Du. (YOU)

"Sie" is the formal version of "you" in German. You would use it when talking to authority figures, most strangers and people generally older than you. "Du" is the informal and you would use it with friends, family and people younger than you.

As an example, "Woher kommst du?" means: "Where do you come from?" using the informal "Du," you would use this when talking to someone at a party, or with a mutual friend. Whereas if you were asking a stranger, you would need to use "Woher *kommen Sie*?" It means the **exact same thing**, which is mildly infuriating because you have to remember the different verb endings for EVERYTHING.

It is also still used a lot in German business. My wife had to address her old boss by the formal version "Sie." To everyone else in the office she could use "Du", but her boss felt it necessary to stay "formal."

In general, there comes a time in most relationships where the boss, or the person you have been talking to will allow you to "Duzen". This is when they give you express permission to use "Du" with them and no longer the formal "Sie".

Warning, you can only do it once you have been invited to use it, using it before the invite will see you corrected back to the "Sie" version – honestly!

I got approached by some kids in the street one night asking me about a football score, they used "Sie" to communicate with me. This firstly, made me feel a million years old and secondly meant I messed up my reply, because I am so used to using "Du", that I couldn't remember the "Sie" responses or figure out if I should reply in "Du" anyway or stick to "Sie" ... Sometimes I really want to give up!

"Gepoopst"

Germans have a lot of dare I say it, ugly words in their language and a lot of complicated words as you will know if you have ever tried to study German. Even the word for sorry is just terrible.

Sometimes though, the German language throws out an anomaly that sounds, well, adorable. I believe this to be in my top 3 favorite German words and in the tradition of childishness; it is the German word for fart.

"Hast du gepoopst?" - "Did you fart?"

What the Hell is an Adverb?

I am currently on an intensive German course. German is not an easy language to learn, unlike say, English.

Germans are very sympathetic to those learning Deutsch and for some, it may not be all that hard. However, it is made infinitely harder for me as I didn't do too well in English at school. So the structure you need to apply to learning German sentence structure, comes from the basic understanding of what a adjective is, a noun, where a verb goes, whether or not it is present perfect, or past tenses.

You will need an understanding of the basics such as indefinite articles, irregular verbs and such, So, a lot of time learning German, has also been spent really understanding English.

Top tip: If you want to learn German, know your English.

Sprechen Sie English?

In general, most Germans can speak at least some English, but they can be shy about it.

When you ask "Sprechen Ze English" a German will always reply "A little bit" then proceed to dazzle you with the amount of English they know.

I find that alcohol also helps their English speaking.

50 Things to Notice about Germany

Food and Drink

Never Tap Water

Despite the fact that German tap water goes through more rigorous checks and testing for quality than bottled water, Germans seem to be obsessed with buying their water.

If you are someone who has spent your life grabbing a glass and filling it to the brim, with cold water from the tap and taking a big gulp, then in Germany you could land yourself in hot water, because nearly everyone here drinks bottled water.

If you are a guest at a restaurant, asking for a glass of tap water with your meal is pretty outrageous, as in DON'T EVER DO THIS.

However, you will find that this is not limited to dining; it also extends to being a guest at someone's home. Nearly every household will be able to offer you; chilled bottled water, both still and fizzy. To not have these on hand would be similar to going to a house in the UK and them having no tea!

Culturally in Germany, bottled water used to be a way of displaying wealth and over the years has simply become culturally ingrained. This means as a citizen of Germany that every week, I have to schlep 12 x 1.5-litre bottles (18kg) of water through a supermarket, out to the car, then from the car up to my 5th-floor apartment, despite having a ready supply of perfectly healthy, fresh, drinking water in my kitchen.

I must admit though, I am now on board with the whole drinking bottled water thing – not bottled still water, that will always be odd for me, but I have become addicted to fizzy water (Wasser mit Sprudel). Flat water doesn't do it for me anymore and I blame Germany.

Fizzy water used to taste gross, probably because you are waiting for that hit of sugar that you associate with a fizzy drink, but don't get, it was bottled disappointment.

Fizzy water now though is my nectar. On a hot summers day an ice cold fizzy water is like heaven on your palate. All that plastic though is not heaven for the environment. Hence the German Pfand system as mentioned already in this book.

Drinking with breakfast

The breakfast table is set, Ham? Check! Cheese? Check! Fresh Bread? Check! Two bottles of sparkling wine? Check!

Wait... really?

Drinking with breakfast has a terrible connotation attached to it in Britain. Wino's and drunks will routinely frequent less, *shall we say,* classy establishments, at 9 a.m., for a cheap breakfast and a pint of ale, but it's certainly not a family affair.

Germans love to drink alcohol, but they do so in a far more responsible manner than Brits and maybe even Americans. Yes, despite the fact Germans drink with breakfast.

Here it is very popular to indulge with a glass of Sekt for breakfast. It is a staple of many family events, like Easter and Christmas, yet it doesn't turn families into raging day/binge drinking alcoholics, as would certainly be the case in the UK.

Whilst a "Sekty" breakfast is the thing I am most familiar with, it is certainly not limited to this. Visit Munich at any time of the year, and all over the city, restaurants are serving a nice glass of Weizen (Yeast Beer,) with peoples eggs at 7am.

I tend to join in this tradition whenever possible, before falling asleep in my soup at lunchtime and waking up with a 2 p.m. hangover.

Tea

Being British, you tend to drink a lot of tea, because tea solves all your worldly woes. Tea gets you up in the morning, gets you through work, takes you to bed at night, tastes delicious and is as traditional a part of being British, as moaning about the weather. Germans also drink a lot of tea, but not tea as you know it.

For a German, drinking tea is somewhat of an event. For example, just order a tea in a restaurant and you will not receive a cup of tea. There are a host of hurdles to get past first! You will be asked: "What kind of tea?"

"Roibush tea? Fenchel Tea? Apfel tea?" "No, no", you'll reply, "*normal* tea."

NOTE: You need to order "Schwarz Tea" (Black Tea) and then because you are not an animal, you will ask for milk and proceed to disgust your host. Germans drink normal tea, without milk. Monsters!

Even in an Irish bar (that I used to work at) you would prepare tea starting off with a "fancy" glass of hot water... not a mug... and place the glass onto a little plate. Then put another little plate on top of the glass, pick up a box FULL of assorted teas, walk over to the customer, place down the cup of water and present the box of tea to him, as if you are presenting a box of riches to an Emperor. Then wait patiently whilst they sift through and invariably ask you for the one tea that the box does not contain.

But it's not just the ceremony of tea. Germans seem to believe that tea has healing properties akin to actual, real medicine.

"Oh, I'm so sick"

"Oh dear" I reply to my wife

"Can I get you some Lemsip?"

"No, it's OK", comes the response

"I'll take some tea."

Despite you reiterating for the millionth time, that essentially you are just drinking slightly flavored water... slightly *badly* flavored water at that, German's will not hear that their "Fenchel tea" is doing nothing that a cup of warm water could not.

In the time it has taken me to type this section about tea, the UK will have drunk nearly half a million cups of real tea. If Germany drank tea to the same extent, they would believe themselves to be impervious to death.

Beer for the lads

Ordering drinks on a night out is generally a straight forward affair. I normally allow my partner to order the drinks for us, due to my lousy German and quite regularly I will allow her to pay as well.

What I have found is, Germany is the only country I've been to in the world where I can repeatedly order a couple of drinks; for instance, a large beer and a white wine, that when the waiter brings you your drinks, he will stop and ask who the beer is for.

"Well sir, the liter of beer is clearly for my small lady here, whilst I sip on that tiny Chardonnay".

Yes, it could be that way round, and in Germany, it's probably quite commonplace, but anywhere other than Germany it is not particularly likely.

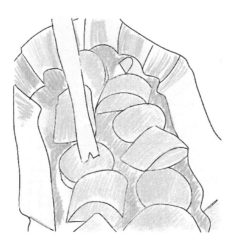

Currywurst

I am a huge fan of German sausage, it's right up there with my favorite things about Germany. One thing I am still not sure if I am very fond of though is Currywurst.

Served by street vendors the nation over, they take a sausage, slice it into small round pieces, cover it in a tomato based, sweet curry sauce, sprinkle it with a tasteless curry powder, then place it on a small paper plate with a bread roll and "voila". You enjoy your sausage with a small plastic fork and a small beer. Generally handing over around five Euros for the privilege.

It is difficult to say what makes a good Currywurst because the sauce can mask a lot of the sausage taste, so this part has to be good. I enjoy mine the most in the winter and would say that this German tradition needs to be tried when in Germany as you will not find this delicacy anywhere else in the world!

Ice Ice Baby

If you are asked if you want to go and get "Ice" by a German, you may do exactly as I did, look vague and repeat with confusion "ICE?"

I am still not used to this word, every time I hear a German tell me "we get some Ice" I picture that we are about to go to a dark street corner to procure the latest class A street drug.

Actually though, Germans mean *ICE-CREAM*! But have efficiently omitted the word "cream" to speed up the whole transaction.

It is a big tradition in Germany to venture out for a walk that ends at a local ice-cream shop, which you will find in pretty much every town, village and high street.

Lastly, when the German you are with asks for "spaghetti ice", don't be confused, it is merely ice cream that is pressed through a machine that makes it all stringy – like spaghetti and topped with a strawberry sauce that presumably is meant to resemble the marinara sauce.

Breakfast

Breakfast on the weekend is a big deal in Germany, and man it is good.

Breakfast – well, what outsiders may call brunch – is where the whole family/friends etc. will sit together and enjoy a breakfast of rolls, cheese, cooked meats, salmon, eggs, good coffee and other delights for around two hours. It may also include one or two bottles of Sekt (fizzy wine,) which leaves you feeling like you want to go straight back to bed after having it.

However, a group walk around the village/town/city usually follows it. I think it is the equivalent of the English Sunday roast, but with fewer calories and effort. Cooking chicken, roast potatoes etc. is a three hour-long marathon.

In comparison, placing lots of fresh cheeses and meats on a table takes less effort, is healthier and allows you time to really enjoy your food, since nearly everything is serve cold already.

50 Things to Notice About Germany
Driving

Die Autobahn

When I was young, the revelation that there were roads in Germany that had no speed limits was incredible to me.

I dreamt of this magical road in Germany where I could drive as fast as I wanted and pledged one day that I would find it. Little did I know at the time that there is actually over 12'000 km of Autobahn in Germany, and a huge percentage of this is unrestricted carrying only an "advisory" speed limit of 130 KMH (81 MPH).

In my experience, the bulk of people from Germany will drive fast on the Autobahn, but incredibly vigilantly and carefully. They generally only pull out into the fast lane if there is sufficient room and are quick to move back into the slower lanes to allow the faster cars to go past. All very polite and efficient.

Someone should have told the Dutch guy I was driving with about the advisory speed limits and driving courtesy on one particularly scary trip I took on the Autobahn.

I was travelling back from Amsterdam to Frankfurt, with a gentleman who was offering a ride on a popular car sharing website.

He kindly collected me and we set off. The trip through the Netherlands was all fine, with nice conversations about Europe. It was in summer and back then, all was good in the world. Until we hit Germany and the Autobahn. It was for him, his first time on the unrestricted roads, in his brand new Audi A4... and he felt it was an opportune moment to put the car through its paces.

What followed was a very, very uncomfortable and scary trip, with much braking and pant wetting, where we more than once topped 245 KMH (152 MPH). We were actually averaging over 200 KMH (120 MPH,) for the majority of the journey and ended up getting from Amsterdam to Frankfurt - some 440 KM, in just under three and-a-half hours.

That weekend journey, was actually me coming back from Amsterdam, having just parachuted for the first time. I honestly don't know which was scarier; the jump, or the drive.

I think the general advice here is, just because you can drive as fast as you want on the Autobahn, does not mean that you should.

REISSVERSCHLUSS System.

The "zipper principle", is one thing I really do appreciate on German roads. It fit's in with the concept that drivers – for the most – part drive in what could be described as an *orderly* fashion.

If you are on the Autobahn, doing 220 km/h and come up on someone doing 200 or so, nine times out of ten, they will move over, out of the lane to allow you on your way.

The same principle applies if someone comes up behind you. You move. Essentially, the exact opposite of what drivers in England do for instance. People in England feel almost duty bound to police the roads, driving for miles and miles in the fast lane at 73mph without moving over. Infuriatingly.

The same "policing" attitude, mixed with English politeness applies in road works where the roads go down to one lane. British people will get into that lane up to a mile in advance. Woe betide anyone who stays in the lane that's closing and tries to merge at the last minute, this is absolutely guaranteed to be met by a string of obscenities and an attempt to stop you from getting in the lane. I speak from personal experience here, as one who has tried to squeeze in and as someone who has tried to stop someone squeezing in.

This is where the Germans again step in to solve that problem. There are two lanes, so you are expected to make use of both of them. Then, where the road narrows to the single lane, it is law to merge in a "Zipper" style, i.e. one after another.

This takes some getting used to for me as a Brit, in the correct lane long before the road merges being undertaken by BMW after BMW (yes it is always BMW drivers, even in Germany) as they merge at the last possible moment.

I was mad about this, until someone told me that it is the law, which hit me all at once, causing me to reply,

"Ohhhh…. well, yes, of course it is, this is Germany."

Washing Cars

German's take a lot of pride in their cars. Why shouldn't they? After all the country produces BMW, Audi, Mercedes and Porsche.

The car is a statement of your social position and wealth in any country, but Germany takes particular pride in the cars that they drive and take good care of them. Which can create quite the spectacle.

Washing your car at home is banned in Germany for environmental reasons. I totally get that. Washing chemicals off of your car into the public water drainage system and wasting water to clean a vehicle is both hazardous and wasteful. But when you factor in the fact that Germans wash their cars three times more often than Brits, you begin to see just how much water they could be wasting and just how many pollutants they would be passing into the drainage system.

What this means is, car washing is big business. Not only for the money it makes, but how it also keeps thousands of low skilled workers in Jobs.

You will notice just how clean the cars are on the roads when you drive around a city, but for me, it's too much.

On a Saturday you might think, "I'll pop to the car wash and give the car its annual scrub." Your mind is instantly changed when you see that the queue for the car wash is over one kilometer long.

I kid you not; some of the most popular car washes have people queuing for hours down the street. The biggest and most expensive car wash in Stuttgart cleans 60 thousand cars a month!

Frankly, I can think of better ways to pass the time and therefore skip the queue and drive by in disbelief as hundreds of drivers waste a beautiful sunny day, sat in their cars waiting for their turn to make their car clean for a few days. Madness!

Winter Tires

Germany has a reputation for being a bit of a nanny state – in that you must conform to various rules and laws in order to protect you, *from yourself*. Whilst these rules and laws are in general a good idea, sometimes they can seem a little intrusive.

Rules like, not trusting you to cross the road by yourself and making it law to wait for the green man before crossing. Or, another rule that I was completely unaware of before I moved here, that they do not trust you to be able to navigate the treacherous German roads of Hamburg, without exchanging your tires twice a year between summer and winter tires. These will normally be marked M + S for mud and snow tires.

Whilst there are such things as "all weather tires" it is far more likely that you will have two sets of not only tires – but wheels. From October to Easter (in German = Oster) so "O to O," you have to adorn winter tires and in the other months, summer tires.

Down in the south of Germany, this does make sense, their weather is far more extreme than say Dusseldorf, or Hamburg.

But the German government, not wanting anyone to feel left out, created a blanket law/rule that applies to all Germans.

There are a few disagreements around whether or not it is LAW to have winter tires on your car between October and Easter. After some research I have found that; it is actually not the law to do it by season, but by weather condition.

Thus, if in the event of an accident, the law will work like this; if you did not have winter tires on your vehicle and had an accident in bad weather conditions, you would be automatically held responsible for the accident. This even applies if you were driving a rental car. So in extreme weather conditions, be sure to check your tires have an M + S mark (Mud and Snow).

So, for every car, there are two sets of wheels and you either store them yourself, or pay a garage to store them for you. And because not every everyone will pony up to afford two very nice pairs of wheels, often in the winter you will see very expensive cars rolling around on horrid steel wheels, as opposed to the "fly" 22" alloys that came with the car.

Which is exactly the case for me, urgh.

Honest Parking

Parking your car on the streets around Germany can be free, but where it is, it's normally time limited.

In your car, you must always possess a little blue disk (pictured above) in your vehicle. When you have parked, you must adjust your disk to show your time of arrival, this is so that any Stadt Polizei (city police) knows what time you arrived and what time you should have departed by.

Returning to your vehicle after two hours and adjusting the arrival time cannot manipulate this infallible system. No sir.

But the German people are far more honest than that and it is not just with parking. Public transportation is set up on a kind of honor system too, whereby you are trusted to do the right thing. For instance, there are no barriers at any train stations. Instead, you are deemed responsible enough to buy a ticket to ride the train. Yes you will see ticket inspectors on some trains, but for the most part, Germany trusts you to be an honest stand up individual.

I would say it's easier to be an honorable person in this country as the public transport costs are very reasonable. Not like in the

UK where you can't get anywhere near a train without first parting with 50 quid... but I digress.

Road "Rage"

Driving through a city such as Frankfurt can be both a harrowing and exhilarating experience. Lanes merge and disappear, traffic appears from your right and expects you to stop, flashy motors both over and undertake you simultaneously.

If you dare to change lanes at an inappropriate time or hesitate at a green light you will most likely experience the German equivalent of road rage.

Instead of hurling abuse, names, and finger gestures – as is widely accepted in towns and cities across the world – Germans are more likely to pull up alongside you at the next set of traffic lights and discuss the inadequacy of your last lane change, or point out how you could drive better.

Of course, this is often delivered through a heated debate, but rarely does it descend into childish name-calling and never into fighting.

Whilst I learn the roads, I also need to learn how to road rage correctly.

Part 3

10 Things I Love About Germany

The first time I came to Germany, I travelled to the south of the country to attend a one week training course for the German logistics company I was working for at the time. I honestly had no idea what to expect. Growing up in the UK, history lessons and old movies would vilify Germany; the war is all that the average Brit knows and it is truly a shame. Because of this narrow view, I was truly expecting the country to be a dark, unwelcoming place.

It was also the first time in the country for my colleague, with whom I had travelled, and after a long flight delay we arrived at the airport, already late and decided that hiring a car, instead of public transportation, was going to be the best way to get to the hotel, some 100 km away.

Germany is full of hundreds of wonderful old castles and estates that have been renovated to accommodate conferences and weddings etc. But they are usually out of the way, a long way from cities. It helps focus the students I guess, because you can't really leave the hotel for the duration. But it certainly doesn't make them any easier to find.

This trip was made before the days of satellite navigation, google maps and international data roaming. So, when we jumped in the car, the only resource available to us for navigation was the hotel brochure. On the back was a tiny five cm x five cm map and some loose driving directions in German.

This map was not really designed for navigation, more for orientation. With no other choice but to see if we could find it, we set off.

This being my first time in Germany, I didn't speak a word of German and had rarely needed to drive on the wrong side of the road. So the immediate experience of sitting on the wrong side of the car, on the wrong side of the road, in terrible weather left me feeling somewhat frightened and disorientated.

I squinted my eyes into the distance every time a road sign came into view, trying to get more time to read every city name. I could see that the town of "Ausfahrt" was to our right. After 30 minutes of driving, I was certain we were driving in circles around this town, it must have been the biggest town in Germany I thought, it went on for miles!

I couldn't see it on the map and I began to get increasingly nervous that we were hopelessly lost. Eventually out of absolute sheer luck, we managed to use the tiny map to orientate ourselves and find the hotel, hours after darkness, late in the evening, much to our relief.

Upon arrival some of our colleagues were already in the bar. I shared with them the story of our nightmare journey and being lost near AUSFAHRT. They were visibly confused.

I exclaimed that every time I thought we needed to get off of the Autobahn, the town was always the same.

It was only then that it became clear. Ausfahrt isn't a town. It's posted on every turn off of the autobahn. It is in fact, the German word for exit.

The German town of Ausfaht,

Since the days of living in the UK and my nightmares of trying to navigate Germany, I have become a lot better travelled.

I have lived in Amsterdam, Frankfurt and now live in a town called Wiesbaden about 60km West of Frankfurt. I can speak a little of the language and while I may not have mastered it, I still do my best to integrate into German society. I do this by partaking in their many traditions and events, eating their delicious Wurst and drinking their delicious Bier. There always seems to be something going on here and it can make you quite fond of life in Germany, speaking of which:

Here's ten things I love!

1. Beer.

Germany has been brewing its own beer for hundreds of years. As far back as 1516, German purity laws were introduced. The law states that beer must contain only three ingredients; Hops, Barley and Water. Most cities and regions have their own favorite beer and all are slightly different. In Bavaria for instance it is a smoky beer that's king. Try a Weizen (Wheat Beer,) when you are parched on a summer's day. It is nectar.

2. Events

Germany is a place where there is ALWAYS something happening, from Flohmarkt's (Flea Market/Car boot sale's) to Wurstfests (Literally Sausagefests - *tee hee*). Every town and city has annual events, where the streets are closed and replaced by vendors selling trinkets, meat, beer and wine - which leads me to point 3.

3. Weinfests

Now these do not take place all over Germany, but I live in the Rheingau, Germany's famous wine region. There are hundreds of Vineyard's only a stone's throw from my city and each year, many of the wine makers have festivals where entire towns shut down to go visit. Wiesbaden and Bad Dürkheim have two of the largest wine festivals in the world and I visit them every year.

4. Christmas Markets

Germany can be a pretty grey place in Winter, it sometimes feels like you go without sunshine from November to March some years. In order to brighten those long winter months, most towns and cities set up Christmas markets. They are truly beautiful. Hundreds of market stalls decorated in Christmas lights, little wooden huts selling wonderful ideas for Christmas gifts and they are not are not even the best part! A nice hot Glühwein (warm mulled wine) keeps the chill off and a nice sausage roasted over an open flame. It's the perfect way to get into the Christmas spirit with friends.

5. The Autobahn

My in-laws live in the north of Germany, a three and-a-half to four-hour drive depending on traffic. In other countries where your speed is limited to 120 kmh, it can take much, much longer to cover the same distance. When you take into account Germany's size and the quality of their roads, you will begin to appreciate why there are no speed limits in places. That being said, they may not be this way forever, there are regular calls from environmentalists and motorists groups to limit speeds on the Autobahn to 130kmh, because one in four road deaths in Germany are attributable to speed.

6. The countryside

The countryside is never far away in Germany and it is a welcome break if you live in a big city. Many cities and towns can have a very similar feel about them; owing to the fact most of them were rebuilt around the same period. But what is unique is the countryside. You have the Black forests, the

Rheingau, The North sea and many other places that are beautiful to visit.

7. Bakeries

There seems to be a bakery on every street corner in Germany. Bread is a great source of pride for many Germans and they have far more choice than a UK bakery. It is also one of the few shops that are allowed to open on a Sunday, meaning that fresh bread for breakfast is the perfect way to start your Sunday morning.

8. Frühstücken

"To Breakfast" is a verb in German and can be a pretty serious affair. Coffee, cheeses, hams, salmon, fresh fruit, vegetables, eggs, wiener sausages and fresh bread, plus don't forget the Sekt. The German breakfast is designed to bring family and friends together for a social breakfast; they can last long into the day, over a period of several hours whilst you catch up on the gossip of the week. It certainly beats a slice of toast and a downed coffee. It is a perfect way to spend a Sunday morning, I can assure you.

9. German Directness

When you first arrive it can come off as rudeness. But it's not. It's just that it's more efficient to give you a direct answer than beat around the bush. After a while you begin to admire the frankness and honesty and your feelings are no longer hurt by it.

10. Diversity

Germany is made up of a lot of cultures, some of which came during the post war period to help rebuild the country and then ended up settling. There are large Turkish and Italian populations throughout Germany, adding to a real melting pot of character. Italian Gelato shops (ice cream) and Turkish Döner places adorn many high streets, even in the smallest of towns. People for the most part respect each other and allow those whom come from other cultures to still retain their cultural identity whilst retaining the German identity and roots.

Part 4
Articles

As well as writing my blog, I have also been a feature writer for Wall Street International, where I have posted several articles about my life in Germany as an expat and different locations in Germany that I have visited, from Berlin to the site of the former concentration camp in Dachau.

Writing was a way of coming to terms with how different my life was becoming from the life I left behind in the UK. Writing large articles really made me focus on what I had noticed, or felt and allowed me to express it. I think they deserve a place in this book. While some are more light hearted than others and some are a little tongue in cheek, the fact they were published by such a widely known publisher has always been a source of pride for me.

Article 1
Seven Reasons I Pine For Home
Autumn, the melancholy season

Ascending to the top of a leafy ravine, the sounds of people laughing down below echo over the noise of my heavy breathing, I can see the smoke from their family fire rise not in wisps and curls, but in a large hanging drift, like the clouds and just as grey.

The leaves, yellow, golds, reds and greens hang lazily in the breezeless air, this hot summer has taken its toll on them and it will not be long until they can retire to earth.

Having lived in England all my life where summer temperatures only average around 22 Degrees, this hot summer in my second year living in Germany, makes me appreciative of my "toil" in the hot seasonal sun. I'll admit this hard work has really been about fun, mainly in the form of exploring, socialising and travelling as still being relatively new to Germany, it is my duty to make the most of the warm season. Summer wine festivals, new friendships and street parties - there is always something amazing happening.

Stood in the forest here in Germany, I am aware of how much I enjoy living in this wonderful country, but there is something about this transitional and sometimes melancholy season that makes me pine for the UK. Given the choice between a grey autumnal British day and a grey autumnal German day, I would choose a British day every time, here's why:

1. Pubs

Germany has bars and restaurants, but nowhere except Britain and Ireland, have real traditional pub culture. The fire crackles at the other end of the pub whilst the bartender makes unobtrusive, lazy small talk with you; "nice day for it" "rains lifted up then?" "Cash or card?" More than enough to make you feel welcome, but not so much that you feel you have to continue a conversation. After all what you really came for wasn't the chat, or the free Wi-Fi, but for the food! Menu's filled with dishes like Beef and Ale pie, Fish and Chips and Toad in the Hole to top off your pint of ale and pat of the pub dog.

2. Familiarity of locations

Considering that I live in Germany, there is always something more I could be doing to integrate with my host society, like learning the language for instance. What I do to make up for my lack of language progression is to integrate through the many festivals, traditions and foodstuffs that Germany has to offer. I much prefer this to bumbling my way through many German lessons.

As a permanent stranger, everything is new and there is so much to be sampled but it can make it difficult to build that sense of familiarity. "Shall we go back to such and such restaurant" "Oh, No, I have read about this other place I would like to try." So off you go to another new experience.

I think with fondness about being back home where you know where everything is; you know that you can go to Westonburt Arboritum this time of year and it will be breathtaking, you know what you will see and how it will feel. You can go to a pub in Aldbourne (a small rural village in Wiltshire) and know that you can order a pint of Bombardier ale, with Beef Wellington and the 20 quid in your pocket will pay for it. You know how long it will take to drive, the best route, when not to leave and more importantly you know how it is going to feel. Living in a foreign country, you get used to everything being so, well, foreign.

3. Sunday Roasts and other soul food

You have "home cooked food" advertised to you wherever you go - it has always bewildered me why restaurants will advertise that it "tastes like home cooked" if I wanted home cooked that day, I would have stayed at home and cooked. Make me something that "tastes like it was prepared by professionals using the finest ingredients and tools". That's why I am paying good money for it after all, but I digress.

The days where you do want home cooked; there is nothing more homely on a dreary autumn day than roasting a chicken, peeling potatoes and spending an afternoon in the kitchen filling your house up with the smell of memories. That sense of familiarity is about as big an escape from continental life as you can get.

4. Friends

Fortunately for me, I never really had a lot of friends and in the summer everybody seems to disappear. Perhaps it's on holidays, family BBQ's or working long hours. Or so they tell me. I have my suspicion that the real reason we all disappear is that there is little to no sports on TV and if we did get together that would mean we would have to make actual conversation.

So, the coming of autumn helpfully coincides with the start of the soccer season, you generally begin to hear from your friends again who want to escape the house now that the days are grey and rainy causing their families to be holed up inside creating a stir craziness that is best cured by sitting in what is essentially someone else's mutual large living room at a pub.

5. Sports on TV

Living in a foreign country and not speaking the language you become a slave to Netflix. There are plenty of sports on TV in the summer but none that anyone really watches, take Tennis for example, name one person who puts time aside out of their diary to watch the tennis? So that leaves, Cricket, Cycling and um, well that's it really.

Autumn in England signals the start of the football and rugby seasons and every shot, pass and tackle will be televised and replayed so heavily that eventually you will have memorized the entire commentary.

6. Duvet days

What I also enjoy about autumn back home is the pace of life. The days are not so hot, bright and sunny that you feel compelled to get up and go and explore. The only reason I get up in the summer is due to an overwhelming sense of guilt and paranoia, that by being in bed I am missing out on something.

At home in this season though, when the mornings are darker it is perfectly acceptable to laze in bed until midday, safe in the knowledge that it is raining too hard and it's too cold outside to do anything. You also know for a fact that all of your friends are doing the exact same thing. When you are lying in on a Sunday at home in autumn, you are not missing out on anything. Quite the contrary, you are doing the very thing you should absolutely be doing.

7. Melancholy

Described as a feeling of pensive sadness, typically with no obvious cause, it is a familiar feeling that autumn really brings it out. For me I begin to feel reflective and melancholic as the nights draw in, the blue skies replaced by grey, the leaves that make everything so virile and fresh, replaced with the naked torsos of trees and bushes alike.

Melancholy is actually not always unwelcome, but after a while you need to shake it off. This is a harder feeling to escape in a foreign land however, because when those "today I feel sad" days come on, you can't immediately indulge your melancholy by feeding it the familiar; by catching a football game at a pub, cooking up some comfort food, or by going to your favorite store to buy some new scarves.

Living in a new and pleasantly unfamiliar land, it's that little bit harder to slip out of, therefore in order for you to enjoy your melancholy, it might pay to have a healthy dose of autumn at home.

Article 2
8 Reasons why you will never learn German

And it's not because you are ignorant, intolerant or rude

Most people that move to a different country believe before they go that learning the language is the highest priority, above everything. However, some, like me for instance, do not and find themselves living in the country for many years without mastering even conversational German.

OK, so before you write your hate comments – let me explain. I have lived in Germany for 3 years and have been married to a German for about the same. I have worked here for the last 2 years and I still haven't learned German. Depending on who you speak to, I am being either extremely ignorant by living in a country and not learning the language, or it doesn't really matter.

As a total disclaimer, I do speak transactional German so I can order food, make an appointment and ask basic questions, but if the response is outside of what I was expecting I am more than likely going to be stumped. Despite this lack of fluency though I love living in Germany – I don't feel isolated, or left out, I don't feel ignorant or rude either for the most part, I do however feel occasionally guilty when I am invited to a party (or my in laws) and all the attendees switch to English just for me… in their country… in their home! But, for the most part it's fine.

So why after 3 years do I still not speak German? Well let me tell you:

1. It's hard

As a native English speaker you are blessed. Blessed with the fact that you speak a global language and you didn't have to spend hours and hours of your mid 20's and 30's trying to master it. German is far more complex a language to grasp basics of than English, with its multiple sexes for words and its formal and informal versions it is a bit like trying to complete a 10'000 piece puzzle when there are multiple pieces that are the same shape, but just different colors and whilst they shape may fit, it's still wrong. The only thing that will get you through this is practice, patience and persistence – even then, if learning other languages is not something you find very natural, then you will likely think it impossible.

2. Germans speak English

Most countries use English as their second language. Meaning that when you travel to most places in the world, you can get by using the hosts limited English to come to a reasonable understanding. In fact, when other countries travel, like an Italian to France they will most likely attempt to converse in English – because it is a global language that is easy to master the basics of. In a lot of foreign countries, a large part of the media they consume is English language, most music in countries like Germany is in English and nearly all students learn English at school so they grow up with a larger exposure. In my experience the younger and more educated the German, the better their English in most cases, meaning that if you get into a conversation with a German they will most likely switch to English, or when you get to your appointment most people will help you along by switching to English. Also, Germans think speaking English is cool.

3. Practicing is difficult

There are apps and books and courses and CD's and meet up groups and friends – the opportunity to practice is all around you – but you still require that old prerequisite of learning: will power and dedication. Lack these and it doesn't matter how many easy to use resources there are, you still are not going to do it. Couple this with the fact that most Germans switch to English at the slightest hint of an accent, it means practicing is hard.

4. Courses are hard to get on

Germany allowed some million or so migrants into the country in the last 2 years and depending on what sources you read, it could almost be double that. As part of a migrant's arrival, they are given a 6 month course in German at the government's expense. As a migrant from another European country you do not receive any priority, its first come first serve and you simply join the waiting list. Most language centres have been overwhelmed by the sheer numbers of students meaning private language schools have been pulled in to help out, this means the quality of your education will vary widely from centre to centre. Currently I am on a 6 month waiting list and have been for the last 6 months, so there you go.

5. I can get by without it

I am a pretty introverted kind of guy, so I don't need large swathes of friends and acquaintances to make me feel like I belong. Also, I work for a large American organization and most Americans speak at least passable English... meaning this has become my social circle. Doing simple tasks with basic German is fine and my wife translates anything more complicated meaning I get by with my A2 level German.

6. It's not fun

Sometimes learning is fun – particularly when you learn something you are passionate about, learning the Ukulele was fun, learning to sing was fun, learning German just isn't fun. Challenging, frustrating, confusing, soul destroying are better adjectives to describe it, if you are a glutton for punishment and have never tried, then try learning a foreign language - personally I would rather go to the dentist.

7. Your focus initially is on arriving or learning your job, not learning German

Learning the language should be your first priority! Oh, really? Not learning my job? Orientating to my new city? Finding somewhere to live? Filling it with furniture? Working out public transport? Or where to buy food? Etc. Learning the language when you first arrive in foreign country is important for many, but it soon loses its importance when you are trying to simply arrive. Couple that with the fact that many people speak English, you may soon realize that learning the language is not the absolute priority you thought it was.

8. My wife translates everything

There's a shortcut for you – find a German wife. I have the conversation about learning German regularly – I would say at least once a week. Sometimes I feel guilty that I don't speak fluent German and everyone around the dinner table, in the middle of Germany is speaking English just because of me, sometimes I feel left out if someone tells a story in German and everyone is laughing accept me, sometimes I hate my inability to grasp another language easily. But 99% of the time, it's honestly not a problem for me, maybe this is a luxury most can't afford, but my wife is fluent in English, my work and my colleagues are American, I speak enough basic German to get by and most Germans speak English, all in all I'm fine without it, you might be too.

My situation is pretty unique and a word of caution to my "you don't need German" tongue in cheek article, if you want to apply for and get a job in Germany, you are going to need at least B1 level German – this is considered fluent. Without a close friend or a partner who speaks the language, just doing the basics may be tough – it will also isolate you to only those Germans who speak good enough English to make any effort to get to know you. When I first arrived and didn't speak any German and it was very hard just taking trains, or going shopping they lead to confusion and frustration. If it wasn't for my wife my attempt at integrating would have failed. Bottom line is, it's hard, but with the basics, you can get by and this leads to increased comfort in your new home country.

Article 3
An indelible scar

A view of Dachau concentration camp

Just as music is the perfect accompaniment for writing, it also serves as a key – nay - vital ingredient for the road trip. But what happens when the recipe is spoiled?

My first road trip in my Mini – my very own Mini adventure - would take me on a path through some of the world's most beautiful scenery, but not before a pit stop at a place where some of modern men's worst atrocities occurred.

So much has been written about the holocaust, the Nazis and the Jews that I am certain my voice contains neither the prose, nor the writing experience to fully convey the humanity and the echo of evil that Dachau near Munich conveys. I will not attempt to do it justice in this short article as there are many books that can assist you in that. But as a newly world traveler, seeing this prior to driving down to a short stay in the alps made an indelible scar on me.

We pack the car with a couple of days' worth of clothes and essentials heading down to the well-known ski resort of Fieberbrunn in Austria. Setting off on a Friday with a playlist full of music and podcasts we set our sights on a small diversion to Dachau, near Munich. This is one of the first Concentration camps built by the Nazis initially constructed as a prison or camp for political prisoners, it developed into part of the Nazi's final solution. All in all through its existence it held 225'000 prisoners of which more than 40'000 were to die there.

Getting out of the car in the car park and taking the short walk to camp, there is an immediate change of mental pace.

After the 100's of Km covered accompanied by music picked specifically to sing along with during the trip is silenced. Out of a form of respect for the place the laughter stops and curiosity takes its place. Not the kind of curiosity that a child might have for exploration or knowing, but a curiosity of how one might feel about what one is about to experience. What will what I am going to see and understand mean to me? How might I react? For some reason the air feels heavier, like if you were to shout, the sound would not travel.

"Arbeit Macht Frei" the gates that mark the entrance to the camp are in themselves fairly unremarkable. What is more remarkable are the remains of the train platform behind where many of the arrivals and prisoners of the camp arrived before solemnly trudging through the gates of the camp. As I pass through the gates I feel a kind of trepidation again that uncertainty of how I will feel about this.

Initially, visually, the place is underwhelming. Your eyes move quickly to the two remaining huts that would have housed prisoners and to the large structure at the other end of the grounds. A looming grey concrete building that looks like some kind of torture chamber dominate your seeing eyes. Unsure where to start, curiosity moves your feet along the fences with the sinister watch towers looking over a guided tour.

Eavesdropping I can hear that they are discussing the neutral zone between the camp grounds and the electrified fence. A zone where should inmates be found, they would be fired upon from the guard towers. A death some would actually opt for during the camps terrible history in order to end their own internal torture.

As we carry on towards the looming grey building, it emerges that this place is actually a church, built to commemorate the dead, as opposed to a torture device, which it clearly reflects - the sentiment is there, but the design only adds to the foreboding feeling in the camp air. Exit to the left over the small stream which, unbeknownst to us led to the cremation house, the site upon which many of the execution's occurred in the camp. The house has been restored and cleaned, almost clinical in its appearance now, it contains pictures within and the descriptions of the rooms leave you in no doubt as to the evil that was perpetuated by the guards and the regime at the time.

If you are blessed with an active imagination, then placing yourself into these situations is soon a curse. The seeing and the feeling of the rooms leaves you tormented with images of horror in your mind's eye. Bodies stacked high, corpses hanging from their ropes prior to being loaded sometimes 2-3 at a time into the ovens for incineration. It is a place where thoughts of anything outside of what you are seeing, imagining and feeling are impossible; you are only consumed by the horror that happened here.

A short walk around the gardens will allow you to see execution pits, graves where ashes were buried and places where bodies were stored prior to incineration. It is where you find yourself asking how this could really have happened, how could this have been able to take place?

Upon returning to the main camp grounds where the prisoners were held, we walk through the open hut that gives you an example of how hundreds of prisoners would have been kept, either up until their deaths, or until liberation - if they were lucky. Some prisoners were experimented on in the hospital huts next to the accommodation, cruel and unusual

117

experiments, it appears no matter what was in store for you at the camp, nothing good, or anything like normal was ever likely. This was not even the worst part.

It is late in the evening before we enter "the bunker" - the camp prison. We are one of the last people left in the camp and the only people in this area, the light is dimming and this dark single story, single corridor building sits unassuming behind the main administration block. Entering through the main door, as would many of the prisoners, you are met by a variety of images and notices about past prisoners, some of their fates, some of the conditions they experienced including; isolation, standing cells and savage beatings, even death.

Staring down the long, dark corridors in the silence a wash of ice filled my body causing me to shiver to my core. The evil that the walls seem to have absorbed radiates back out to you in the echoes of every footstep.

It got under my skin, my breathing shallowed as my pupils struggled for light down the dim corridors, in my imagination the place was alive again, the pain, the suffering; the anguish was reverberating through the structure. It was too much for my partner and she left the building, leaving me alone with my morbid curiosity, my body soaking in the unusual feelings, and sounds that were not there, but I could hear.

Tiptoeing along the dark corridor as if not to disturb the air with my own presence less it awaken repressed energy from the walls, investigating the small cells that remained open with text projected onto the walls from ex-prisoners, true quotes and stories from inmates adding flame to the fire of unease. Exiting at the end of the long corridor into the dim twilight my unconscious mind makes involuntary shudders, ridding myself of the energy absorbed from this evil feeling place.

We soon leave the camp in silence, the toll of our new understanding making us feel heavier in some way. An overwhelming sense of loss and helplessness brings up questions such as how, who and why. Knowing that these atrocities occurred within living memory of some is the hardest part for me to comprehend - billions of years of evolution and this happened within just a few generations.

Continuing our journey in silence, we both look out of the windows before reaching back for some music to help distract us, but now it feels like playing dance music at a funeral and nothing seems suitable. We plunge back into silence again. The next words are from my wife around an hour later when she points out the Alps. "Fucking Hell" is my actual response. I have never seen the Alps and just as nothing can prepare you for the feeling of experiencing a Nazi death camp, nor can anything prepare you for the breathtaking beauty of the alps in Autumn for the first time.

After our weekend and on the way back home I am exhausted from what I have seen, the pendulum of emotion swings on its spectrum; from the worst of humanity, to the best of nature. A new symphony of powerlessness and insignificance has been added to my life's soundtrack.

Article 4
Berlin.

Built for efficiency not for affection

When I think back to a past visit to Prague, my memory gives me an overwhelming sense that I have seen something incredible - the beauty, history and architecture. When I think back to Paris, my memory serves up a feeling of grace, elegance and cultured romanticism. When I think back to London I remember the ceremony, tradition and hustle and bustle. When I think back to Berlin, I think of, well, actually, I can't quite put my finger on it.

Arriving on a wet Friday at the incredibly modern and shiny "Hauptbahnhof" (Main Train Station) everything was just how it should be albeit with a curious sterility. There are trains, shops and many tourists as you would expect, but when you step off the train at Milano Centrale, London Paddington, or Paris Gare du Nord, your first breath fills you with an immediate sense of the city. Millions of people have walked before you through these buildings that were built to be noticed. Train stations are the historic gateways into cities and were designed to be grand and impressive. In Berlin, I got a sense that this was distinctly German - in that it was built for efficiency, not necessarily for affection.

Berlin is a young city, even younger when you think that it has only been unified since 1990. In fact, if I am honest, I do not believe that I ever truly understood the magnitude of the Berlin Wall and its impact on the city until I visited what is left of it.

Visiting the Berlin Wall Memorial on Bernauer Str. you will read stories about "defectors, escapers, spies and snipers" that bring to life what is now unthinkable in a modern, unified Europe. Much of the city was obviously destroyed in WWII, so aside from a visit to the Berlin Wall, touristic buildings of historic importance are harder to come by. When the city was rebuilt, it was done so without much affection towards its past. You will of course on any visit take time out to see the Reichstag, where the German Parliament sits, then there's the Brandenburg Gate and the Victory Column, but then what?

I'm sure many Berliners will feel justified in screaming at their computers citing buildings of note I have failed to mention, but from my point of view, had I gone to Berlin just to see the sights then I would have left disappointed. I suggest you have to dig deeper. For me Berlin needed to be felt, in order to really experience it. Luckily for me, we happened to discover the Mauerpark.

Taken from the Mauerpark "Situated in what was once the militarized "death strip" of the Berlin Wall (or Mauer) that divided East and West, Mauerpark is now a social, cultural, and artistic center of the city."

Visiting Mauerpark on a Sunday is like visiting a hipster's paradise. Not only do you have the park, but also a "Flohmarkt" (Flea Market) and hundreds of stalls selling knick-knacks, clothes, trinkets, music and treasures from all over the world. Catering stands cook up delicacies from all cultures such as, Japanese fish, Mexican Burrito's, Turkish Falafel, and French Crepes, something for every taste. Once you have tired of this (or you run out of Euro) you can visit the Mauerpark proper and I am sure that my experience will not be very different from yours.

Stepping through into the park, I first noticed a large gaggle of people gathered around a 3-piece band. They were playing amazing funky rock with electric instruments and amplifiers, hooked up to an old car battery. On the other side of the park stood an amphitheater built into the hillside, where a large audience was watching a street performer. Between here and the amphitheater, the park was littered with small groups of people dancing to music, cooking out, enjoying the first glimpses of spring and soaking up the friendly atmosphere that's laid on by the cosmopolitan people of the city.

This was the Berlin I had heard about, but in the first two days of my visit had just not discovered. Leaving the park a few hours later to catch the train home, I think I understood Berlin for the first time. It's about easygoingness, acceptance of individuality, and embracing it. Just in this one park, it was all being physically demonstrated through art and culture by the people.

My memory of that day, of all those people in the park is enough to make me feel like I belonged there. It is no longer a memory of a rather disappointing visual tour around Berlin, now it is a memory about the excitement, curiosity and envy that others get to permanently live amongst it. Berlin may have been built for efficiency. But affection for it, has been built by the people.

Thank you for reading this book. I hope that it fills you with a sense of excitement about Germany and if you are visiting, travelling through or moving here, I am sure you will grow to love the country.

Printed in Great Britain
by Amazon